MIMESIS
INTERNATIONAL

POLITICS

n. 22

REFUSING
TO BE SILENT

Engaged Conversations
with Leading Intellectuals

Edited by
Zona Zarić and Gazela Pudar Draško

This publication was supported by the Ministry of Education, Science and Technological Development of the Republic of Serbia.

Reviewers
Petar Bojanić
Snježana Prijić Samaržija
Vedran Džihić

Translation and proofreading
Edvard Djordjevic
Sophie Galabru

TABLE OF CONTENTS

SPEAKING FOR THE WELLBEING OF SOCIETY

MOBILIZATION AGAINST FEAR

IN SEARCH OF NEW WORDS

VOICES FOR THE FUTURE

SPEAKING
FOR THE WELLBEING OF SOCIETY

NEW HORIZONS OF SOCIAL CRITICISM
Michael Walzer

Michael Walzer is a prominent American political theorist and public intellectual. Professor Emeritus at the Institute for Advanced Study (IAS) in Princeton, New Jersey. He is the co-editor emeritus of Dissent, a left-wing journal of anti-imperial orientation. As one of the most prominent American political theorists and globally recognized social critics, his contributions include a revitalization of "just war theory" that insists on the importance of "ethics" in wartime – condemnation of slavery, genocide and crimes by states involved, that represent a minimum for every state to respect and follow. To date, he has written 27 books and published over 300 articles, essays, and book reviews in Dissent, The New Republic, The New York Review of Books, The New Yorker, The New York Times, Harpers, and many philosophy and political science journals.

You have recently said that "political intelligence and moral sensitivity work much better than ideology, and it is these two that should guide our choice of comrades and our decisions about when and how to act abroad." How come this applies to international relations, but not to individual countries?

It does apply to domestic as well as international politics, but I have found that political commentary, on the left at least, is usually (not always) more intelligent and more sensitive when the subject is local. Commentary on foreign policy tends to be more ideological. Consider, for example, the arguments about US imperialism and the leftist demand for US disengagement. Plausible enough in some cases, but not in every case. I believe that it is most important to think hard and concretely about conditions in this foreign country and that one and to talk to the people who have the most at stake. One example that I have used more than once in arguments about foreign policy: the Iraqi feminists who didn't want the US to withdraw, as we did withdraw in 2011, because that would leave them exposed to deadly attacks from the sectarian militias. American leftists weren't listening, as we should have been. But we have to listen to feminists at home.

Our current president loves to quote Max Weber as a justification for all government misdeeds, implying that dirty hands and immoral acts are an integral part of politics and that he is the one who suffers the most for having to get his hands dirty. However, in your seminal article on the topic, you write that Weber's solution of the dirty hands problem "within the confines of the individual conscience" is "neither possible nor desirable" and that a more public solution is necessary. Could you expand on that?

I wrote that article a long time ago, but I will respond to this question with an example from recent times. I don't believe that the use of torture by the US government after 9/11, in the course of "the war against terror," is an example of the necessary but immoral acts that I wrote about. These acts of Bush, Cheney, and company, were immoral and unnecessary, and the proper political response was exposure, condemnation, and an unequivocal commitment not to act this way again. But suppose that one of the cases involved the much discussed "ticking bomb" in a school building and a prisoner who knows which school. Getting the information from the prisoner is really necessary, and immoral means may also be necessary. So, let's say, the prisoner is tortured—what then? What I want is a public and plausible account of the necessity and a reaffirmation of the immorality. The people who ordered the torture should tell us: This is what we had to do, but we are not proud of having done it, and we know that our hands are dirty and that we have to find some way to make them clean again.

Some philosophers teach my dirty hands article in introductory classes as an example of intellectual incoherence. How can the right thing to do ever be something that it is always wrong to do? I continue to think that's just the way it is.

The U.S. government has just hosted talks between the Serbian and Kosovo delegations in Washington D.C. The dispute around Kosovo is yet another struggle over land that has both real and symbolic meaning for the sides involved. Territory has not lost its significance, in spite of huge migration flows and technological changes that make us closer on the global level. How do we think about this?

Despite the large scale migrations and the huge refugee populations, most people most of the time want to be in a place where they feel at home, a homeland where they have a history, where they can visit the graves of their grandparents, where they know the landscape. Cosmopolitan intellectuals have been too quick to separate themselves from all this and then from the great majority of their countrymen and women, who will never be citizens of the world. People like me, people who live on the left, need to find a way to defend the idea of a homeland and at the same time insist that this defense doesn't require a cruel and exclusivist nationalism. I've been arguing for a much more generous immigration policy for the US, and that is (partly) because I believe that the immigrants will come in and, like my grandparents, make a home here. They may feel nostalgia for their old homes (though my grandparents didn't feel nostalgic about czarist Russia), but if we welcome them and put them on the road to citizenship, America is sure to be their children's homeland. That's true of other countries, too.

History seems to show that building a desired society requires some degree of violence. Could we speak of a balance between justice and violence in producing desired change? What is acceptable and what is not?

I should begin with skepticism about revolutionary violence, which usually ends with the revolutionaries killing each other—and a lot of other people, too. Defensive violence can be justified, only that. When the American colonists declared independence, the British sent an army and the colonists had to fight for their freedom—that was justified. Terrorist attacks on the families of British loyalists would not have been justified. Terrorist attacks on French civilians in Algeria in the late 1950s, the bomb in the café, were not justifiable; indeed, the choice of terrorism foretold the horrific politics of Algeria later on. The fight for justice is best conducted through mass mobilization, general strikes, civil disobedience, for these are forms of struggle that point toward a democratic politics.

In the last decade, we have seen that many modern democracies have become fragmented and divided societies. How do we envision and defend pluralism in the era of fake news and manipulation through social media feeds? How can we build a political culture where criticism is not understood as a drawback, but a necessary part of the process towards better politics, or even better political solutions?

I am not "on" the new social media, and the problems they have produced will be dealt with, one way or another, by people the age of my grandchildren, not by me. But pluralism has a history, and it is possible to reflect on how it came to be accepted in those places where it was accepted. Think about the fragmentation produced by the Protestant Reformation, or about the ethnic and religious diversity brought about in the US by mass immigration, or the cross-class politics that made the glorious years of social democracy possible. In cases like these, it wasn't plurality alone that made for pluralism, but also mutual recognition and coalition politics. The different groups had to realize that danger to one was a threat to all. Repress the Baptists and the Methodists will soon be in trouble. Repress the Irish and the Slavs won't be safe. Repress the workers and the petty bourgeoisie will feel the pinch. Today's identity politics is often an effort to go it alone: make a lot of noise, play the victim, and argue for your "rights" as if they are just yours and no-one else's. Sometimes, at least, I understand the impulse, but that kind of politics won't work. Diversity won't be good for anyone unless all the diverse men and women acknowledge each other's rights and work together.

Should leftists embrace religion and how?

If they are unbelievers, they can't "embrace" religion, but they can try to understand its meaning in the lives of many people. Speaking only for myself, as a liberal Jew, I have chosen to engage with the religious tradition in a partly critical, partly appreciative way. The aim of the project I've worked on for many years, with colleagues in Israel, "The Jewish Political Tradition," is to figure out what parts of the tradition need to be revised, rejected, forgotten, or revived for the sake of a decent politics in these latter days. It is important for anyone attempting a project like this, in any religious community, to be at once respectful and critical. Rigidly orthodox or fundamentalist believers won't acknowledge the combination, but many religious men and women will, and then a dialogue can begin.

Finally, you supported the Institute for Philosophy and Social Theory in Belgrade in its struggle to preserve its autonomy. It seems that critical thinking is under attack throughout the world. How do we create new horizons for fighting back?

Autonomous institutions like your Institute (and mine in Princeton), and learned societies and professional associations, and journals, magazines, and newspapers, are absolutely necessary if there is to be a culture of criticism. Criticism needs protected space. Of course, people can criticize from exile or write letters from prison, but a rich culture of intellectual and political engagement, of argument and, sometimes, polemic, can only be the work of people who feel secure at least with each other and safe in the places where they work or the living rooms where they meet. Even the authors of *samizdat* need friends. So, what we have to do to "fight back" is to cling to our friends, defend each other, and refuse to stop writing and speaking. It won't always work, not in the time frame we hope for. It is dismaying to watch, for example, the closing down of Hong Kong's freedom. How should we respond? By welcoming the exiles and giving them space to work and by never forgetting the names of those in prison. And by speaking out ourselves and rejecting every ideological excuse or apology for the oppression. The new horizons of criticism actually have a long history.

Interview conducted by Gazela Pudar Draško

THE UNIVERSITY AND CIVIL SOCIETY
Jonathan Wolff

Jonathan Wolff is a British philosopher and academic. From 2012 to 2016, he was Professor of Philosophy and Dean of the Faculty of Arts and Humanities at University College London. Before that, he was the secretary of the British Philosophical Association and held the position of editor and then honorary secretary of the Aristotelian Society, which publishes *Proceedings of the Aristotelian Society*. After eighteen years he resigned the post of Professor of Public Policy at Oxford University to become a member of the gambling law revision government committee. Since then, his carrier has taken a different path – reflecting on disadvantage and equality, and also on public policy decision-making, considered essential for the welfare of citizens, through the cooperation as well as confrontation of opinions between policy makers and academics. In addition to being a regular columnist for the *Guardian*, Wolff is the 2021 recipient of the Institute of Philosophy and Social Theory of the University of Belgrade's *Miladin Životić Award* for critical engagement. His books include *Robert Nozick: Property, Justice and the Minimal State*, *Why Read Marx Today?*, *An Introduction to Political Philosophy*, and with Michael Rosen he edited an introductory reader to political philosophy.

In your recent article in the Guardian, you claim that universities need to step up as central pillars of civil society. In the UK context, that means rethinking the higher education system. However, in Serbia, this acquires an additional meaning. Serbian academics are often exposed to open attacks in the media for their critical stance against the authoritarian regime. Intellectuals should come

down from their ivory towers, but public engagement should still
not end up in politics. Can you comment on this issue?

Every context is different and I wouldn't like to generalize.
Although much in higher education needs to be rethought, my
argument in the Guardian was more about university leaders being
prepared to enter public debate, and stand up against all attacks on
civil society, and not merely to lobby for their university's own
immediate interests. It's a delicate balance in any society, and
it's especially difficult to criticize government when you are so
dependent on government decisions to keep the sector flourishing.
If, for example, the government threatened the universities that
higher education funding would be reduced if leaders publicly
oppose some government policy, then there is a real dilemma. At
times like this wide solidarity is needed so the government comes
under widespread criticism if it acts in an arbitrary or vindictive
way. More likely, everyone will keep their heads down and try to
protect their own interests. But my main argument in that article
was intended more at university leaders than intellectuals.

The role of intellectuals, and especially those who have a
public audience through their academic work is slightly different.
Some academics are gifted with the ability to make an important
intervention in public matters more or less instantly, others need
months of reflection. I find myself somewhere in the middle and
am reluctant to state a view on a controversial matter without
some time for thought. But inevitably if you say unpopular or
uncomfortable things you will get attacked. In my own case I've
escaped lightly, but colleagues – especially female and minority
colleagues – have received death and rape threats. Of course, these
are likely to be from people who have no intention to carry them
out, but you never know. And all around the world academics are
losing their jobs, or even being sent to prison, for their criticism
of government. Not everyone has the courage to speak out on
an individual basis, but it seems to be incumbent on all of us in
academia to show solidarity, especially when we can do so with
little personal risk.

You have served on several public policy committees, some linked to the medical profession, currently in focus due to the pandemic. What is the experience and a contribution of a philosopher in this milieu?

When a philosopher is included in a public policy committee it can be hard to find a clear role or purpose. For example, if the philosopher has spent their life defending a moral or political theory then might think their job is to persuade the rest of the committee of the truth of that theory, and to deduce a policy recommendation on the basis of that theory. But this is very unlikely to work; why should the rest of the committee endorse that theory? Or the wider public and policy makers? It is better, in my view, for the philosopher to help to show how the policy issue involves values as well as other economic, pragmatic and legal concerns, to bring those values to the surface, and facilitate informed debate about how to achieve a balance between competing issues. These philosophical skills, rather than any particular doctrine, is, in my view, how a philosopher can make the most helpful contribution.

Would you call yourself an engaged philosopher?

I have used the term 'engaged philosophy' for what I do, but I realise that it's ambiguous. For some it means politically engaged, thereby arguing from a particular ideological point of view. That's not what I mean. Rather I mean that in looking at ethical issues we should start not from grand theory, but engage with the issue in front of us. We should try to understand the public debate and why it is a matter of concern right now. We need to look at details of law, policy and regulation, the history of the problem, and what is done about it in other countries. In other words, we should start with the concrete and move to the abstract, rather than thinking that abstract thought will alone be enough.

In Ethics and Public Policy: A Philosophical Inquiry, *you investigate the link between assumptions and policy development, or how moral disagreements influence political ones. How should we mitigate or eliminate bad influences?*

That's quite a question! There are many types of bad influence, from conspiracy theories, to cognitive errors, such as confirmation bias (only looking for evidence that supports your view). Confirmation bias affects us all, and we don't think of it as bias, for it can look like rigorous research, to back conjecture with evidence. In my view the way to avoid bias and inadequate research is to find experts in the field who can tell you what the important, influential and controversial areas are in their area, rather than relying on internet searches and so on. Things that look obvious or at least highly plausible in theory may not reflect how the world actually works. Common sense is a very bad guide in social science. So, my advice in policy areas is, wherever possible, to find as much empirical evidence as possible, and to start with changes that can be modified or reversed if they don't have the intended effects.

There is a strong feeling, confirmed by numerous studies in the Balkans, that citizens distance themselves from politics, perceiving it as a dirty business, with little to no real expertise required or involved. On the other hand, the expectation is for highly educated people to step into politics, in order to improve its level of morality – for the sake of citizens. What do you think could be the first step in overcoming clientelism and corruption, which is supposed to bring citizens back into (better) politics?

This is such a hard question. Hannah Arendt pointed out that when people who are not used to politics are drawn into political issues, they often don't have the discipline of listening to contrary arguments, and assessing evidence, but may well follow a charismatic leader uncritically, dismissing criticism as irrelevant, or motivated by sinister interests, or even close to treason. You can respond to this in several ways: try to keep politics an elite activity; try to educate the people into the nature of mature political debate; try to enthuse a counter-movement; and so on. This is one of those areas where structural factors seem more important than individual motivation. Corrupt structures reward corruption, clean structures reward behavior with integrity. But structures need to be changed by individuals, and ultimately, we need heroes who are prepared to try to change corrupt structures, rather than merely penalize corrupt officials (which of course is necessary too).

Do we need more education, or more different education? What is the path towards a society of equals?

I would never say that we don't need more education. And I would never say we do everything right in education. And I think a society of equals is a far-off dream, whether or not it even makes sense. I'm particularly exercised about whether it will ever be possible to abolish all unjustified group hierarchy. My goal is more modest: to identify the worst inequalities in society, and for theorists to work with activists to fight injustice on many fronts. This will mean different things in different societies, but almost everywhere there are highly marginalized and excluded ethnic or religious groups, the rights and interests of people with disabilities are ignored, some struggle to feed their families or have any type of human life, and one disadvantage tends to compound into others that blight lives. There is much, highly important, work to be done, in cooperation with others. Social scientists are needed to provide an accurate documentation of harm and abuse, philosophers to bring out the values engaged, and talented activists and lawyers to agitate and advocate for change. I would say coordination of efforts is, at the moment, a greater challenge than education or knowledge.

Interview conducted by Gazela Pudar Draško

INTELLECTUALS SHOULD NOT SPEAK FOR OTHERS, BUT WITH THEM
Catherine Malabou

Catherine Malabou (born 1959) is a French philosopher and feminist. She is Professor of Philosophy at Kingston University, at the European Graduate School, and in the department of Comparative Literature at the University of California Irvine, working on the relations between philosophy, neuroscience and psychoanalysis. Central to Malabou's philosophy is the concept of "plasticity" (the ability of the human brain to remodel itself from not only a lived experience, culture or education, but also from trauma) which she derives from the work of Hegel as well as in light of recent neurobiological discoveries on epigenetics. Author and co-author with Derrida *La Contre-allée (1999) Que faire de notre cerveau? (2004) La Grande Exclusion, l'urgence sociale, thérapie et symptôme/ Changer de différence, le féminin et la question philosophique (2009) Sois mon corps* with Judith Butler *(2010)*, and *Self and Emotional Life: Merging Philosophy, Psychoanalysis, and Neuroscience* (2013).

The guiding thread of your work seems to be the concept of plasticity and the possibility of a plastic ontology. Plasticity denotes both the capacity to "take form (as in the plasticity of clay) and to give form (as in the plastic arts and plastic surgery)" as you specify in your book Changer de différence, Le féminin et la question philosophique *(Galilée, 2009). Originally, you have introduced this concept through an analysis of Hegel's work in your thesis, under the supervision of Jacques Derrida,* The Future of Hegel: Plasticity, Temporality and Dialectic. *When it comes to working, thinking, or living in general, plasticity isn't about adapting to change at all cost – it's about holding oneself open to new ways of being? Can the concept of plasticity transform philosophical discourse into performance? Or offer transcendental conditions for thought?*

You are totally right to say that plasticity is not flexibility. Plasticity designates change and malleability, but it also implies the existence of thresholds of resistance. Once formed, the marble of a sculpture cannot get back to its initial form. A flexible material on the contrary, can be bent in all directions without resistance. It is important to insist on the fact that plasticity is the operation of shaping life, that also sets limits to this shaping itself. A form is not chaos, but a structure, which does not mean that it is rigid and immobile. In this sense, I agree that plasticity can play the part traditionally assigned to the transcendental, but we have then to admit that the transcendental itself is exposed to change — as I tried to demonstrate in my book *Before Tomorrow, Epigenesis and Rationality*. Kant says, in *The Transcendental Deduction*, that there exists, "as it were, a system of epigenesis of pure reason." Epigenesis, as we know, refers to the gradual, plastic formation of the embryo. It might then be possible to envisage a certain plasticity of the transcendental.

Performance? This is interesting. For me, the most interesting form of plastic performance is Nietzsche's eternal recurrence: the movement of life returning to itself. *Ecce Homo* can undoubtedly be read as the first philosophical performance which puts at play, in the form of an autobiography, the way in which life returns to itself, like a ring, at every birthday. Remember the beginning of the book: "On this perfect day, when everything has become ripe and not only the grapes are growing brown, a ray of sunlight has fallen on to my life: I looked behind me, I looked before me, never have I seen so many and good things together. (…) How should I not be grateful to my whole life? And so I tell myself my life."

Eternal recurrence is a circular movement, that accomplishes something, this is why it is a performance. Nevertheless, every turn of this return produces a difference. This is its plastic aspect, that should be more often recognized.

What do you think of the continental/analytical philosophy split? Is the division and opposition of these two traditions largely a matter of technique? Could we hope to look at it in the words of Richard Rorty "as an unfortunate, temporary breakdown of communication?"

I don't think this split to be temporary, nor explicable in terms of breakdown of communication. "Philosophy" is a name comparable to what medieval thinkers used to call "universals," that is, general and void terms that could apply to different and even opposed realities. I do think that "philosophy" is one of them. Continental and analytical philosophers share nothing, have nothing in common. Philosophy, then, is just a name for two incompatible realms. This is not to say that some bridges are not possible sometimes, Paul Ricœur built a lot in his books, in admirable manners. Nevertheless, no one has ever succeeded in finding a way to create genuine and fertile encounters between them. It will perhaps come one day. Recently, speculative realism has been an interesting attempt, but I am not sure of its success.

In your latest book Le plaisir effacé. Clitoris et pensée *(Editions Payot & Rivages, 2020) you state that one of the greatest challenges of our time is the defeat of domination. You use the clitoris as an attempt at deconstructing this need for domination whether on an interpersonal or sovereign level. As the clitoris is an organ solely intended for pleasure, it does not serve for reproduction, nor for maternity, it does not seek to dominate. Synonymous of a sexuality without penetration nor reproductive aim, it allows to think of a power without domination. What kind of power would this be? And how would it enable a paradigm shift?*

In this book, I stated that the clitoris was an anarchist because, as you say, it is the bodily inscription of another relationship to pleasure that does not rely on penetration or reproduction. Anarchism recognizes that there exists a specific problem of power, a problem that exists on its own. The specific problem of power is precisely domination. This problem is not only economic, not only political, but also domestic, institutional, academic, and/or psychic. It pertains to the love for the master. As we know, psychoanalysis offers a method for confronting and working through certain issues important to anarchism, such as the sexual mechanisms of submission to and acceptance of authority, the attraction to death, or the psychological mechanisms of state power. Which is not to say that psychoanalysis itself is exempt from the disavowal of anarchism, but this is another story.

It is clear that anarchism is not only an anti-state movement, the destruction of the state is not even its primary goal any longer, anarchism is first and foremost a question about the mechanisms of domination that, once again, extend far beyond the political. These mechanisms work at both the collective and individual levels. The great anarchist activist Emma Goldman complained that most radicals, radical feminists in particular, paid attention only to the "external tyrannies" while the "internal tyrants," operating in small circles, even in one to one relationships, remained unexamined and undefeated. In *The Tragedy of Woman's Emancipation*, she declared: "The explanation of such inconsistency on the part of many advanced women is to be found in the fact that they never truly understood the meaning of emancipation. They thought that all that was needed was independence from external tyrannies; the internal tyrants, far more harmful to life and growth--ethical and social conventions--were left to take care of themselves; and they have taken care of themselves. They seem to get along as beautifully in the heads and hearts of the most active exponents of woman's emancipation, as in the heads and hearts of our grandmothers."

Domination, or illegitimate authority happens when one person is constantly subordinate, and gets prisoner of such a situation.

In my book, I tried to show that the clitoris was subverting authority. It is a significant characteristic of anarchist thinking, that domination can be challenged, fought against, overthrown even, by external forces, but that it also possesses, at its core, an internal line of fracture, a crack that allows for its self-subversion. I think that we are witnessing today a great number of resistance acts against the infeudation of feminine pleasure to submissive patterns.

In the concept of consent, we understand the abdication of the woman in the face of male desire; she consents rather than initiates, she abdicates rather than resists. What are the limits of the concept of consent when it is used to justify this or that sexual violence? Imposing consent as a form of sexuality that is well lived and free only leads to a very damaging representation of sexual relations in which women "consent" because they would lose something in the sexual act. Consent, in this context, seems very much linked to this conception of a sexuality oriented towards male pleasure, which would take the woman's body as its object. Obviously, it is a fundamental legal and pedagogical tool that can allow for greater protection of women, and especially children, from sexual violence. But from a theoretical point of view, doesn't this concept prolong something like a denial of a powerful and fulfilled female sexuality?

I totally agree that consent is a pernicious notion that distorts its own meaning so to speak. In the notion of consent is normally contained that of a freely accepted involvement, gesture or action. It has been twisted in a horrifying way to exonerate the authors of rape, by saying that the victims were consenting. So that the rape was in fact a quasi-normal sexual intercourse. Consent has ended up being twisted against itself. The great feminist Gisèle Halimi was one of the first lawyers to deconstruct this notion, and she won some famous battles against rapists. Thanks to her, rape was considered a crime, and not a misdemeanor any longer. You are perfectly right to say that this term now is a disavowal of feminine desire.

In 2010, you co-authored a book with Judith Butler entitled Sois mon corps *(You Be My Body for Me), an interactive cross reading of Hegel's* Phenomenology of Spirit, *in particular the implication of the body in the master/slave dialectic. This dialogue puts into play your respective concepts of "plasticity" and "performativity." What do they have in common?*

Let's start by recalling that in *The Psychic Life of Power*, Butler develops a very interesting and profound analysis of the relationship between the master and the slave, or bondsman. She says that the master implicitly addresses the bondsman the following injunction: "You be my body for me, but do not let me know that the body you are is my body." The operation of bodily substitution is denied by the master. The master claims to be able to detach himself from his own body but denies, in so doing, that he is only transferring it to the slave, asking him to be his body in his place while disavowing this very demand. Butler adds that there must be a certain kind of exchange though, a bargain or deal between the master and the bondsman.

The slave places his body at the service of the lord and so, as it were, turns his own body into the lord's body, but disavows this operation as well, thus becoming "complicit" with the master's disavowal. The "contract" in which the bondsman substitutes himself for the lord is immediately "covered over and forgotten." Bodily substitution then becomes a performative exchange of identity. It is perhaps the law of every bodily identity, to be a product of performativity. A body is always an incarnation of norms coming from outside and implicitly accepted.

I do agree with this, but I think that there is always room, in this performative subjection, for plasticity, that is a transformation of the contract. In order to demonstrate it, I borrow the notion of self-stylization from the later Foucault. There is always something non-performative in the performative, a margin of creation, of a fashioning that is always prior to being.

You have written a beautiful foreword to Anne Dufourmantelle's book The Power of Gentleness *(Fordham University Press, 2018), as you refer to it "a book "about" gentleness written "by" gentleness itself - a book where gentleness is simultaneously subject and object." Against a society that crushes human beings through consumerist logics, this book seeks out revolutionaries, such as Gandhi who invented new ways of resistance and endurance in gentleness, in order to demonstrate that the acceptance of our fragility leaves us incontestably stronger than denying or fighting it ever would. What is the dialectic and the ethic of gentleness?*

I had never thought of gentleness as a philosophical concept before reading Anne's book. It opened a world to me. I had sympathy for this notion, that I understood in its ordinary sense of tenderness, care or light touching. I was totally unaware of its political and religious sense. As the title of the book indicates, gentleness does not entail passivity. On the contrary, it has a genuine capacity to transform life. Let me just quote the book, out of sheer pleasure: "The simplicity of gentleness is misleading. It is an active passivity that may become an extraordinary force of symbolic resistance and, as such, become central to both ethics and politics. Gentleness is a force of secret life-giving transformation linked to what the ancients called potentiality.

In our day, gentleness is sold to us under its related form of diluted mawkishness. By infantilizing it our era denies it. This is how we try to overcome the high demands of its subtlety— no longer by fighting it, but by enfeebling it. Language itself is therefore perverted: what our society intends to give the human beings that it crushes "gently," it does in the name of the highest values: happiness, truth, security.

From listening to those who come to me and confide their despair, I have heard it expressed in every lived experience. I have felt its force of resistance and its intangible magic. In mediating its relation to the world, it appears that its intelligence carries life, saves and amplifies it."

The ethics of gentleness is clear I guess: it is a mode of attentive welcoming. By "attentive," I mean that it guides those who are welcome. It is not just an openness, it is also a way of orienting the other toward her deepest self, to reconcile the other with herself, to make her aware of all their possibilities. I am not sure that there exists a dialectic of gentleness. What might be the contradiction of gentleness, its negativity? There would be an interesting confrontation to develop between gentleness and plasticity...

The Anthropocene, a term coined by Paul Crutzen and Eugene Stoermer in 2000, remains subject to widespread interpretation and debate. In its simplest form it refers to the geological epoch in which we currently find ourselves, one in which humans have a significant and lasting impact on ecosystems. It also describes the techno-scientific character of our post-industrial era and the manner in which human thought, habits and cultures have been organized. Is the Anthropocene a void concept, impossible to phenomenalize or can it paradoxically be an attempt at thinking ecology and politics differently?

I would say that the Anthropocene is difficult to grasp conceptually, as it has, as you said, too many different definitions, and is assimilated to too many diverging moments in history. As you say, what is the start date of the Anthropocene? Based on atmospheric evidence, some scientists consider it starts with Industrial Revolution (in the late eighteenth century). Others link this term to earlier event, such as the rise and development of agriculture and the Neolithic revolution (around 12000 years BP). Some others even propose to extend Anthropocene back to many thousand years, in order to make it closely synchronous with the current term Holocene. The term clearly lacks a convincing unity. But I don't agree that it is impossible to phenomenalize. Precisely, if we understand a phenomenon as what manifests itself, as what appears, then it is easy to see a proliferating number of examples and proofs of climate change. The Anthropocene is perhaps something that can precisely only be phenomenalized, and not conceptualized. There might also be another reason for this.

Anthropocene, as it names indicates, is the era of "man," and the human influence on land use, ecosystems, biodiversity, and species extinction. It then means that a part of the biosphere (the human beings) is responsible for the degradation of the four spheres altogether. How are we to conceptualize this relationship between a part and the whole? The part played by the human as both an agent and a patient?

As the historian Deepesh Chakrabarty affirms, the human being cannot become aware of itself as a natural force, which is precisely the meaning of the Anthropocene: how the human has become a force of transformation of nature as powerful as those which provoked the passage from one geological era to the other. How can consciousness integrate this mineral, geological side of itself? It is impossible. There will perhaps always be a gap then between the theorization of the Anthropocene and its empirical experience.

Do you believe that intellectuals can make a difference and if so, what kind? I am curious to know also what is, in your opinion, the role and place of intellectuals in contemporary societies and in social struggles?

I remember Sartre's definition of the intellectual (perhaps he even invented the term!). The intellectual, he says, is a 'technician of practical knowledge', someone who applies universal practices to particular situations. His mission is to educate by bearing universal truth and values. Unhappy consciousness enables him to show solidarity with the underprivileged (proletariat) class; to advise them, to seek out truths on their behalf, to sign petitions to advance their cause and so on. Are intellectuals still in such a situation today? Can they still believe in their power of mass emancipation? Of course not. First because the "masses" can speak for themselves, second because it is not certain that intellectuals themselves know what meaning emancipation can have.

Nevertheless, as Gayatri Spivak demonstrates in *Can the Subaltern Speak*, a certain type of representation of the speechless voices is still expected from the intellectuals. The intellectuals don't have to speak for the others, but with them. I do believe this function is still absolutely fundamental when it comes, as we said to start with, with domination.

Interview conducted by Zona Zarić

WHAT'S THE POINT OF SOCIOLOGY IF IT IS NOT PUBLIC?

Michael Burawoy

Michael Burawoy is an internationally recognized British sociologist who teaches at the University of California Berkeley. Michael Burawoy has been a participant observer of industrial workplaces in four countries: Zambia, United States, Hungary and Russia. In his different projects he has tried to illuminate – from the standpoint of the working class – postcolonialism, the organization of consent to capitalism, the peculiar forms of class consciousness and work organization in state socialism, and, finally, the dilemmas of transition from socialism to capitalism. Over the course of four decades of research and teaching, he has developed the extended case method that allows broad conclusions to be drawn from ethnographic research. The same methodology is advanced in *Global Ethnography*, a book coauthored with nine graduate students, which shows how globalization can be studied "from below" through participating in the lives of those who experience it. No longer able to work in factories, he turned to the study of his own workplace – the university – to consider the way sociology itself is produced and then disseminated to diverse audiences. His advocacy of public sociology has generated numerous debates. Throughout his sociological career he has engaged with Marxism, seeking to reconstruct it in the light of his research and more broadly in the light of historical challenges of the late 20th and early 21st centuries. He was President of the American Sociological Association (2003-4); President of the International Sociological Association (2010-14); founding editor of the ISA magazine, Global Dialogue (2010-2017); and locally, Co-chair and Secretary of the Berkeley Faculty Association (2015-2021).

Back in Zambia, where you obtained your master's degree in social anthropology, you were already a Marxist. Did your thesis at the University of Chicago, a place rather hostile to Marxism, which is also the cradle of the famous Chicago school, the interactionist approach and the participatory observation method build in reaction to the ambiance and the structuro-functionalism. It is very interesting that in your thesis, which was published and became the book that made you world famous: Manufacturing Consent: Changes in the Labor Process Under Monopoly Capitalism, *you used two competing elements: methodological tools of the Chicago School, and the interpretative framework of the French structuralists, as well as Gramsci, Poulantzas, etc., thus confirming and de facto developing heterodox Marxist theses. This approach was rather original and innovative at the time. You did your research in a factory and closely observed the behavior of the workers in this factory, seeking to answer, among other, the question: Why do workers collaborate in their own exploitation? The idea of consent was central to your analysis. Could you briefly describe this process of consent manufacturing among the workers that you demonstrated in your thesis?*

Yes, I obtained an MA degree in social anthropology from the University of Zambia. I believe I was the first. But you have to understand my teachers were three brilliant Marxists – a Dutch anthropologist trained in the Manchester School, a young Indian anthropologist from the Delhi School, and a renowned South African anthropologist and political scientist, also a committed member of the South African Communist Party in exile in Zambia. They instilled in me a materialist view of the world that was quite consonant with postcolonial Zambia and its reliance on the export of copper. In those days (1968-1972) sociologists in the Third World were as likely to be Marxists as not.

With this baggage I arrived in Chicago in 1972 as a PhD student. I was horrified by the provincialism of the sociology program; its faculty largely ignorant of the world beyond the United States, let alone Africa. With a few exceptions this was all so boring after the exciting seminars at the University of Zambia. As you say the hostility to Marxism in the sociology department was palpable. I began by continuing my research on Africa, especially a Marxist analysis of the then seemingly flourishing racial capitalism of South Africa. Chicago participant observation, such as it was, seemed very backward, still insisting on the insulation of field sites from broader economic and political forces as well as from history. So, I was not only opposing the theoretical frameworks of symbolic interaction, but advancing a very different methodology that I had first learned from social anthropologists in Africa – the extended case method. Of course, theory and method cannot be separated, each feeds the other.

It is important to note that while I was working at Allis-Chalmers (1973-74), Harry Braverman published his famous book, *Labor and Monopoly Capital*, a revision of Marx's theory of the labor process in *Capital*. Braverman traced the transformation of the labor process over the last century to the separation of conception and execution, the separation of mental labor and manual labor. It was an analysis of objective processes as though the subjective response of workers could be read off from the compulsory relations of work. I showed that this was far from being the case with workers able to exploit inevitable spaces in the organization of work. They – and I too – were creative in constituting work as a game that had its own rewards, simultaneously securing and obscuring the appropriation of surplus labor. Together the labor process and the political apparatuses of production resulted in "manufacturing consent."

Workers actively responded to the alienating character of work by working harder and in that way the day passed more quickly and there were emotional rewards to be had at the end of the shift. Moreover, workers collectively ensured that each followed the rules of "making out," so it was difficult to avoid being incorporated into the game. There I was, like everyone else, keen to "make out," even as a Marxist, I opposed this enthusiastic delivery of profit for capital. Practice trumped theory!

How do you see contemporary Marxism on two levels: 1) the one that concerns its relative strengths in relation to other doctrines in

*the academic sphere – do you see an evolution in recent years in
this matter and what are in your opinion the potential indicators to
measure this evolution; furthermore, what is the link between the
weight of academic Marxism in the hierarchy of doctrines and the
relationship of strength between social forces in class struggles
and political forces in political struggles? and 2) the other level is
rather that which concerns its theoretical apparatus and its ability
to give adequate analytical answers for the understanding and
necessary changes in today's social world. In this respect, is a
renewal of Marxism perhaps necessary in relation to the evolution
of current capitalism and, if so, in what directions?*

More difficult questions! The last 30 years has seen a retreat of
the Marxist academic renaissance of the 1970s. As the university
becomes subject to market forces so pressures are applied to
students, teachers and researchers alike that undermine the earlier
collective and radical effervescence. One might expect there to
be rebellions against the university – and there have been from
time to time in many places in the world, not least in France –
but in most countries of advanced capitalism the inhabitants of
the university have been channeled into the pursuit of individual
careers. As at Allis-Chalmers the structures of the neoliberal
university have effectively organized consent to privatization and
corporatization of the university – a shift from the "university in
capitalist society" to the "capitalist university." Marxism has been
in abeyance, out of sync with the dispositions of the times, but, of
course, it has not disappeared. Marxism remains an inspiration to
younger generations who have been involved in social movements
– Occupy, Indignados, Arab Spring, etc. – both inside and outside
the university. There has been a new flourishing of Marxist
periodicals in the US, attracting a new generation.

And where is Marxism heading? Indeed! Influenced by 20
years studying socialism in Hungary and postsocialism in Russia
– again as an ethnographer - I have drawn on the ideas of Karl
Polanyi's *The Great Transformation* that call attention to processes
of commodification rather than exploitation, focusing on exchange
rather than production. Marxism has tended to look upon markets

as functional for capitalism as a process of intermediation that obscures the true character of production. Too little attention is paid to the experience of commodification, especially the commodification of what Polanyi calls fictitious commodities (labor, nature and money, and I would add knowledge) which when commodified in an unregulated way not only lose their use value but destroy society in which they are embedded.

The dynamics of capitalism creates crises of profitability and overproduction that, in turn, drives marketization as a solution. Indeed, I claim there have been three waves of marketization, the latest being neoliberalism that still shows few signs of abatement. The spreading and deepening of marketization – whether we talk of climate change, pandemics, refugees, rising precarity, finance, etc. – is so destructive of human existence that it is more likely to lead to "counter-movements" than the experience of exploitation. Steady exploitation has become a privilege of a contracting labor aristocracy, facing rising precarity. I have proposed the incorporation of Polanyi's ideas into Marxism – rather than the abandonment of Marxism for Polanyi!

Before becoming president of the International Sociological Association, you set up a global sociology project within American sociology, aimed at making American sociology – which was very closed off – more globalized, even in relation to global sociology. In your opinion, what exactly is global sociology? Is it really possible, given the existence of such a diversity of sociological traditions, not only theoretically across national borders, but also when it comes to different geographical areas and even different countries?

Ha! Yes, spending so much time in other countries I could not but become aware of how US sociology defined the parameters of sociology globally by virtue of its control of immense material and symbolic resources – through its powerful (highly ranked!!) universities, its prestigious (very impactful) journals declared to be "international" even though they subscribe to theories and concerns that are peculiar to the US. And, of course, it has the incredible advantage that English has become the lingua franca of the academic world. There have been attempts to pluralize US sociology, and the movement to "decolonize" US sociology have made some inroads. But you are correct that dissolving US hegemony may leave us with factional sociologies with no general coherence. Southern sociology a la Raewyn Connell has its attraction but no theoretically organized center; it exists only as a critique of Northern hegemony.

The question is this: can we pluralize sociology while retaining an inner coherence? Can we include different national experiences to deepen and enrich sociology without fragmenting it? I like to think that the International Sociological Association plays such a constructive role, especially in its many research committees.

We should perhaps distinguish between a global sociology and a sociology of the globe. If we take the ideas of Karl Polanyi seriously then I believe that the response to third-wave marketization has to be of a global dimension. Whereas sociology has conceived of the world through a national lens, as made up of national containers, that will no longer suffice. We can see this most obviously in the case of COVID-19, national solutions can only work so far, but it applies equally to the control of finance capital, refugees, climate change and so much more. The fate of the world is at stake.

You argue that sociology is perhaps the only social science – especially when compared to economic science or political science – that is capable of fighting the dominant ideology because its foundations have always been anti-utilitarian. As a sociologist, I am ready to believe this, and it is clear that among sociologists we may maybe find more heterodox and dissidents than among other researchers, but it seems to me that it is a bit too optimistic to consider sociology as a dissident social science? Since its institutional foundation, the dominant currents in sociology have always been more pro-system than against. It is well known that Emile Durkheim, for example, to whom we are grateful for the institutionalization of sociology, founded his sociological project around the idea of strengthening the theoretical foundations of the

Third Republic in France; and he is not an isolated case, it is rather the rule. What, in your opinion, are the main challenges that sociology, or I should say: critical and progressive sociology, should confront?

Yes, Durkheim is conventionally seen as a rather conservative figure. But once Marx was allowed into the canon, we got all sorts of radical readings of Durkheim. Suddenly people started reading Book Three of the *Division of Labor in Society* through a new lens. There he writes about the three abnormal forms of the division of labor and argues that only by eliminating inequality of unnecessary power (giving workers an independent material existence to establish a relation of reciprocal interdependence with management) and inequality of opportunity (eliminate the inheritance of wealth and that would include cultural as well as economic wealth) can the division of labor lead to organic solidarity! And then if we read the second preface to the same book, we find Durkheim writing about the expropriation of private property and transferring it into the hands of occupational associations. He is proposing a form of guild socialism. Now he may not have been keen on social movements for socialism – they were a sign of a social malaise – but he did have a utopian view of the future, one that goes beyond social democracy, to include what we would today call universal basic income as the only way to assure equality of power between managers and workers. He had a very radical utopian vision of the future. Marxists might well ask about its feasibility and, indeed, its viability, but that would be a case of the pot calling the kettle black!

Weber is a trickier customer. While he is focused on the retention of bourgeois democracy with limited accountability to the demos, still his idea of "vocation" – pursuit of a goal as an end in itself but without guarantees, does create a space for a measure of self-realization. He even writes that time and again the realization of the possible only comes about through the pursuit of the impossible. The task of sociology as a vocation is precisely, then, to formulate the impossible that expands the realm of the possible. Indeed, I would say that sociology lies at the intersection of the utopian and the anti-utopian, the pursuit of possibilities within constraints and thereby loosening those constraints.

But I do think that the troika of Marx, Weber and Durkheim needs an injection of something new. For me that would be the life and work of the great African American intellectual, W.E.B. Du Bois (1868-1963), who brings a new vision of sociology. When brought into a conversation with Marx, Weber and Durkheim, Du Bois generates a new sociology – global, historical, reflexive, attentive to race and class, rooted in lived experience, utopian as well as anti-utopian. He offers us a rich catalogue of exemplary studies including sociological fiction, historical as well as ethnographic studies. His magnum opus, *Black Reconstruction in America* (1935) was way ahead of its time. In my view he is the greatest public sociologist to have walked the earth. Bringing him into the canon – if canon there be – would make sociology exciting again – as long that is as we think of the canon as defined by antagonistic and dynamic relations among its members rather than some monolithic, imperial project.

Shortly after becoming president of the American Sociological Association (ASA), you started the project for public sociology with the idea that sociology could and should intervene in the public sphere. This sparked a considerable debate within American sociology. Would you say that you are an engaged intellectual? Or is that a pleonasm? In the same way a public intellectual is, a linguistic construction that doesn't even exist in France, for example, because being defined as an intellectual implies being publicly engaged. Could you explain the difference between the American and French type of intellectual?

Actually, the public sociology project began when I was chair (together with Peter Evans) of my department at Berkeley (1996-2004). I asked my colleagues what vision of sociology we represent. We came to the conclusion that, in the context of the US, Berkeley sociology was an engaged sociology – my colleagues authored books that captured the imagination of audiences way beyond sociology. Even though I was a Marxist I was certainly not one of those public sociologists, I was a critical sociologist, dangerously veering toward professional sociology. I became an evangelist for public sociology when I was elected President of the American Sociological Association and that, indeed, attracted a lot of attention and controversy that continue to this day.

In my vision of public sociology, I was very much inspired by my South African friends and colleagues who developed a distinctively engaged sociology in contesting apartheid and in particular in contributing to the development of an African labor movement through the 1970s and 1980s. With the lifting of the boycott, I returned to South Africa in 1990 for the first time since 1968. It left an indelible impression on my sociological habitus, so that when I was President of the ASA I would even write about South Africanizing of US sociology!

Now, of course, as you say, in South Africa as in so many other countries, the idea of a "public sociologist" only leads to puzzlement. What's the point of sociology if it's not public? Sociology, by definition, is public! Well, not in the US, where the discipline is so professionalized that most of us spend most of our time talking sociology to other sociologists, writing sociology for other sociologists. Indeed, to talk of public sociology is very threatening to my professional colleagues who fear it will become "pop" sociology, losing its academic credibility. Others were critical of my endeavor as they thought I was trying to smuggle Marxism into sociology under another name. So, the idea of public sociology is, indeed, a very American idea that competes with professional, critical and policy sociologies. This perhaps reflects the expansion of the US university and the way it is organized but it also speaks to the anti-intellectualism of US publics.

No intellectual in the US would receive the celebration and notoriety of Bourdieu, Sartre, Foucault, etc. did in France. Such fame is reserved for Hollywood Stars like Arnold Schwarzenegger. On the other hand, I do recall how Foucault used to love visiting the Berkeley campus, which he did on a regular basis, because as he used to say, he loved the intellectual engagement which he wouldn't and couldn't find in the more sterile French University system, even in the Grandes Écoles. He probably saw only the best side of the US public university, insulated from a degraded and commodified public sphere.

Although I'm not a regular contributor to the media or an organizer in the trenches of civil society, I do consider myself a public sociologist in my capacity as a teacher of sociology. Here I don't compete with other media or disciplines but have a captive audience of some 200 students. I treat them as a public, that is individuals who are not empty vessels into which I pour pearls of knowledge but students who come with their own theories of how the world works based on their own diverse experiences. Public sociology here develops through a dialogue between students and teacher, through shared texts; a dialogue among students about their divergent and emergent understandings of who they are; and, in the best of all worlds, a dialogue between students and wider publics to whom they bring sociological questions and ideas. That's my idea of what I do, students may have a very different view! Another utopia that has to confront anti-utopianism.

Finally, you have been active in many initiatives fighting for democracy and freedom. One of the last ones was for the Serbian Institute of Philosophy and Social Theory, where you joined the international call for support that brought some positive results. Do you believe that intellectuals can make a difference and if so, what kind? I am curious to know what is, in your opinion, the role and place of intellectuals in contemporary societies and in social struggles?

Yes, intellectuals do sign lots of petitions, especially as regards issues of freedom and social justice. There are intellectuals of the right but they are still a minority. It's difficulty to know when such limited participation makes a difference, but one feels compelled to do it whatever the consequences. However, it's often as easy for the powers that be to ignore a petition as it is for dissenting intellectuals to sign one, but they do give moral support to victims of abuse, so that they realize that their fate is being followed across the globe.

I think we can do more than that. In these times when ideas of a feasible and viable alternatives are overwhelmed by the durability of capitalism it is important that sociologists keep open what Erik Wright called "real utopias," concrete imaginations of possibilities that challenge capitalism, potentialities of well-chosen existing institutions and organizations existing in the interstices of capitalism, often generated by capitalism as a means of its survival. Wright scoured the earth and came up with such examples as participatory budgeting, cooperatives, Wikipedia, universal basic income. He would talk to the practitioners, develop an abstract scheme of their principles, contradictions, conditions of possibility and dissemination and then orchestrate public debates that involved academics and practitioners. Here was the best of public sociology in action, forging a global community of real utopians, giving hope to each other as they partake in uphill struggles in the trenches of civil society.

Interview conducted by Ivica Mladenović

RELATIVIZATION OF SCIENCE AND TRUTH DURING COVID-19
Petra Gehring

Petra Gehring is Professor of Philosophy at the Technical University of Darmstadt, Germany, and a member of the evaluation committee of the German Science Council. Since 2014 she has been a member of the Council for Information Infrastructures of the Joint Science Conference (GWK) of the federal and state governments, and its chairperson since November 2017. In April 2020 she took up the position of heading the Hessian Center for Responsible Digitization based in Darmstadt. Her scientific work focuses (among other) on the philosophy of technology, biotechnology and digital technologies, she is also known for her work on power and technology relations, and in her recent book, About the Physical Power of Language. Studies in the Speech Act (2019), she speaks of words as weapons. Her other books include What is Biopower? Of the Dubious Added Value of Life (2006); Inside the Outside – Outside the Inside. Foucault, Derrida, Lyotard (1994); and (with Andreas Gelhard) Parrhesia. Foucault and the Courage for Truth.

When considering the COVID-19 pandemic, it would seem that political intervention into life and death has become more intense than ever. In what ways does the pandemic influence society? Are we witnessing the birth of a new paradigm of the political?

I would be careful not to overestimate the consequences of the current pandemic. Lockdowns do not automatically lead to a sudden love of police states. Most people can distinguish very well between sanitary helpful protective measures and state repression. Perhaps the COVID crisis will make us even more aware of this distinction. Furthermore, it has brought about a deepening of the rift between reality and political rhetoric. It is impossible to embellish reports of patients lying in the hallways of overcrowded hospitals and dying together with their healthcare staff.

Its global dominance notwithstanding, the pandemic is but one of the threats we are currently facing. There is intense discussion about the harmfulness of the 5G network, not always based on reliable information, as a portion of the public seems to be losing trust in expert knowledge. How do you perceive the ethical aspects of new technologies? How can citizens trust experts, if they are constantly facing relativizations of truth and "alternative facts?"

This is a serious problem. Not because we shouldn't critically discuss new technologies – on the contrary. However, "alternative facts" themselves exhibit a downright religious truth claim: "Trust no one, there is probably a great conspiracy behind everything." That is a self-righteous, potentially fanatical position. One wants to be smarter than the experts. Hence, followers of relativizations and alternative facts often circulate in closed communities of mutual validation. Science and technology cannot provide "ethical" conclusions to this phenomenon. What experts for their part should *not* do is to act dogmatically, as possessors of truth. Scientists produce (improvable) knowledge, no more and no less. Engineers solve problems and develop products. Whether it's the right problems and products, no one can decide on the spot. This is why we are politically obliged to patiently discuss issues.

Reflecting on new technologies also confronts us with the question of real-life experimenting with surveillance, a field in which China, with its social credit system based on tracking individual behavior, is clearly leading. Considering the relation between technology and power, could we say that the growing perception of science and technology as mere tools in the hands of those in power will necessarily lead to a growing fear of innovations? Should we fear the development of intelligent (and other) technologies for their potential to support societal control? Are we, as citizens, scientists, consumers etc., capable of coming up with a way of living that will allow us to coexist with new technologies, without compromising our basic rights and liberties?

Surveillance technologies are weapons. Whether it's centralized or decentralized systems of digital surveillance, whether they are in the hands of the state, a clan, or the mob – we have every reason to fear powerful digital technologies when applied to these ends. The so-called intelligence of the algorithms, however, is just one side of the problem. The other is the collecting of data traces: the traces we are producing ourselves, by giving out personal information. It is indeed a question of our way of life: How can I live without constantly thickening the data cloud that makes me socially transparent on all levels? Unfortunately, we are inclined to trust the idea that technology is simply about providing us with intelligent servants. The convenience of using technology, promises of safety, or even occasional feelings of omnipotence (for instance, with "individualized" solutions) – we as consumers are easily won over by such offers. I often find myself wondering what *is* so appealing about remote controls, or wirelessly communicating things, or a smart home. OK, they are considered trendy. But it's the provider who always wins, not the customer. The flip side of individualization is identification.

You were among the initiators of the recent campaign supporting the Institute for Philosophy and Social Theory in Belgrade and the appeal to preserve its institutional autonomy, which was signed by over 500 leading intellectuals from all over the world. It is a matter of growing consensus that the regime of Serbian president Aleksandar Vučić and his party is getting increasingly autocratic, repressing citizens' liberties and withholding information on the actual extent of the epidemic in Serbia. In contrast to Germany and other EU countries, Serbia has introduced extremely restrictive measures against the spread of COVID-19. Do You find that the pandemic offers a chance for the so-called new autocracies to stabilize and strengthen their regimes? Or could this crisis weaken their power in the long run?

Possibly both. The importance of good systems of health care and social security, the indifference of viruses to sugarcoated proclamations... These are lessons we are learning worldwide. Concealing knowledge for longer periods is hard, especially when it comes to exact numbers. The incredibly stupid statement of US president Trump that high infection rates are due to (excessive) testing has unintentionally shown that even autocratic rhetoric is not immune to embarrassment.

Let us take Serbian president Vučić as an example for new autocracies; for a long time now, the local public has perceived him as someone who systematically uses research to optimize his public performances – their tone, dynamics and narration – in order to achieve compliance in his audience. One feels that by complying one is contributing to an important cause for the country, but in reality, one is rendered completely passive as a citizen. This aestheticization of politics causes both passivity and resignation. How do you view this phenomenon, which is not only typical of Vučić?

Resignation is an understandable reflex. Helplessness in the face of absurd circumstances, to which one must adapt since there is no other option – that is enough to drive anyone mad. As a reaction, we withdraw into private niches. Nevertheless, we never resign only for ourselves; we are also stipulating that nothing will change for others either. In this case, philosophy can serve to remind us of a simple thought: we have but one life; and we are living it neither alone nor without obligations. Also, our dreams are not limited to passive consumption. Do we really want to remain mere spectators of what is happening (or not happening) in our common political space? Understanding that not everything is simply fate is the premise of science and technology, as well as of democracy and a good life.

Interview conducted by
Željko Radinković and Gazela Pudar Draško

MOBILIZATION AGAINST FEAR

POPULISM,
A SYMPTOM OF NEOLIBERALISM
Eric Fassin

Eric Fassin is a French sociologist, and currently one of the most engaged left-wing intellectuals in France. Professor of sociology at the University of Paris 8, Saint-Denis and a researcher at the *Institut de recherche interdisciplinaire sur les enjeux sociaux*. From 1989 to 1994, Fassin taught at Brandeis University and NYU, after which he became professor of sociology in the Department of Social Sciences at the École Normale Supérieure in Paris. He also served as a contributing editor of *Public Culture*, a scholarly journal published by Duke University Press. His research focuses on contemporary sexual and racial politics in France and the United States and their intersections. Fassin is author of *L'inversion de la question homosexuelle* (2005), *Droit conjugal et unions de même sexe: mariage, partenariat et concubinage dans neuf pays européens* (with Kees Waaldijk, 2008) and *Le sexe politique. Genre et sexualité au miroir transatlantique* (2009). He advocates for a return to the question of class and winning over abstainers, and is diligent in exposing systemic racism in French society, while supporting anti-racism movements.

The world has witnessed massive protests as a response to yet another case of racially motivated police brutality in the USA. Is this a step towards a more equal society in the USA?

The mobilizations against racism and police violence in the United States and throughout the world are a powerful sign of democratic vitality for at least three reasons. The first is that instead of violent riots, like in LA in 1994, or throughout the 1960s in many cities, these are peaceful protests – even more so than in Ferguson in 2014.

Democracy is on the side of demonstrators. Violence is on the other side. The second reason is that the discourse of race is central in far-right discourses: Donald Trump's political rise starts with the "birther" movement that claimed Barack Obama was not born in the United States (and therefore barred from becoming President). But today, we have a vocal counter-discourse on race: anti-racism in reaction to racism. The third reason is that this is a social movement that mobilizes many young people of all colors and origins. This can give us hope for a more democratic future than our neofascist present.

You follow closely American and European events. How come Europe is monitoring what is happening in the USA, but not much reflection is seen on the other side? A very similar case took place in France: Adama Traoré's death was caused by police brutality. How does France react to its own racism?

Police violence against Black and Arab youths in working-class neighborhoods is not new; nor are strong mobilizations in reaction. Until recently, however, their political echo remained limited in French society. But today, this is changing. There are several reasons. One is that many incidents are now documented (thanks to smartphones), and the information circulates widely (thanks to social media). Another is that police brutality has spread widely: since 2016, social movements against neoliberal policies have also been the target of this State violence – students, unionized workers, and of course the "yellow vests." It is true that the president keeps denying the problem. Emmanuel Macron has declared that "rule of law" makes words such as "police violence" or "repression" "unacceptable." But this denial is becoming more and more… unacceptable – except for the far-right, which is supposed to be the President's main rival.

Recently, you have charged president Macron with being anti-intellectual when blaming academia for bringing racist practices into the public. Intellectuals like you are found "guilty" for "spoiling the youth" and inducing "secessionist threat." Is there a tension between universal values of the French republic and racial practices with deprivation of particular vulnerable (racial and ethnic) groups?

In French public discourse, the rhetoric of color-blindness has long served to blind the majority to racism itself. But today, this has become patently absurd, as so-called Republican universalism has been appropriated by the racist far right. Alas, many mainstream politicians and journalists still use it – not so much these days against the far-right activists, but against the "new antiracists." The former now avoid talking about "races," while the latter use the concept of race to fight color-blind racism. The ultimate irony is that you have neofascist polemicists on TV accusing the antiracist youth that mobilizes against systemic racism of being racist. But on June 13, the multiracial crowd that gathered at the *Place de la République* for Adama Traoré and other victims of police violence spoke the universalist language of rights – equality, justice and truth.

How do you explain the notion of anti-white racism? In Serbia, we can often hear that majoritarian Serbian people have the least rights, that everyone else has priority. This is particularly visible when talking of Roma and migrants from the Middle East. There were similar declarations in France also.

Racism, like sexism, or homophobia, implies domination – which works one way, not the other. You can talk of masculine domination – not feminine. Heterophobia does not make any sense. In the same way, when you belong to the dominant group, you cannot claim to be the victim of so-called "anti-white racism." Majority groups are not equivalent to minority groups; this is true by definition, since both "majority" and "minority" are defined by their position in power relations. Whites are not barred from jobs or housing; they are never exposed to police violence because of their skin color. Of course, they can encounter hostility; but this hostility does not resonate with everyday experiences of structural inequality. Talking about anti-white racism is just another form of denial, as if racism were color-blind!

The relation of the left to the notion of race and racism was somewhat always ambivalent. On the other side, we are facing appropriation of the political correctness on the far right in Serbia.

A neofascist movement that ran in the last parliamentary elections in Serbia had a Roma person high on its list, as a "shield" towards accusation of being fascist and pro-Nazi. How clear can we be on racism and political ideologies today?

In the cartoon South Park, there is one black character, named "Token." In English, the irony is clear: a "token black" is the exception that confirms the rule. Racism is not about individuals. Nazis sometimes had a Jewish friend. In France, today, racists generally have an Arab friend. Neofascist play the same game: in Brazil, Jair Bolsonaro's new minister of education, Carlos Alberto Decotelli, is black. Is that going to make his regime less racist? Of course not. It does not fool anyone – except those that want to blind themselves to racism, and whom we can therefore call racists.

Post-communist Europe has deep resistance towards migrants. What motivates such resistance in countries without a colonial past?

Xenophobia and racism are not just a legacy of the past. They are also symptoms of our neoliberal present. This is why, in Europe, they are not specific to countries like France or Britain. In the same way, Islamophobia is not limited to countries with large Muslim minorities. Racism and xenophobia have little to do with their targets; but they speak volumes about racists and xenophobes themselves. Today, neoliberalism redirects anger against class inequalities to fuel resentment that targets groups such as refugees.

President Vučić has presented himself as Angela Merkel's best pupil, imposing austerity and "protestant work ethics." He has established close ties with Viktor Orban, and is copying his tactics of hijacking democratic institutions. Macron has also undoubtedly been supporting him. You strongly oppose the idea that neoliberalism is opposed to populism. It seems that the regime in Serbia proves you right. How can we recognize this codependence? Is this the scenario of only right-wing populism?

We have been told that so-called right-wing populism was a misguided response to neoliberal post-democracy. On the contrary, I have argued that populism is a symptom of neoliberalism – which is why, in my view, left-wing populism is not a good strategy. The reason is simple: Margaret Thatcher's famous mantra was "There is no alternative!" Indeed, most social democrats have come to accept this so-called "realism." The result is that voters cannot see the difference between neoliberals from the right and (supposedly) from the left. The ultimate consequence is thus the rise of neofascism: if there is no difference between right and left, democracy is empty. If there is no alternative, then, there is no choice – and therefore no democracy. This is why we have to fight to give meaning to the opposition between right and left.

Finally, you have been active in many initiatives fighting for democracy and freedom. One such recent struggle was for the Serbian Institute for Philosophy and Social Theory, where you joined the international call for support that brought some positive results. Do you believe that intellectuals can make a difference and if so, what kind?

Even intellectuals can have doubts about the political importance of intellectual work. Aren't there more concrete forms of activism? But the virulent anti-intellectualism that resonates, for example, in campaigns against the so-called "gender ideology" (or in France, against "racist antiracists" in academia), is a reminder that fascists themselves do care about intellectuals. They are among their favorite targets. Why? It may be because we embody the possibility of critical thinking, which is the opposite of blind obedience. It does not take things for granted. Nothing is obvious; nothing is a given. Maybe what is most important about what we can do is not the answers we give, but the questions we raise. That may be what is most "unacceptable" both for neoliberal and for neofascist regimes. Conversely, that's what democracy is all about: questions.

Interview conducted by Gazela Pudar Draško

COSMOPOLITANISM AND POPULISM
Seyla Benhabib

Seyla Benhabib is a Turkish-American philosopher, an affiliate faculty member in the Columbia University Department of Philosophy, a scholar in residence at Columbia Law School and also a senior fellow at the Columbia Center for Contemporary Critical Thought. She was Professor of Political Science and Philosophy (ethics, politics and economy) at Yale from 2001 to 2020, and before that professor and dissertation director at Harvard. Benhabib is well known for her work in political philosophy, which draws on critical theory and feminist political theory. She has written extensively on Hannah Arendt and Jurgen Habermas, as well as on the topic of human migration, "porous borders," identity and cosmopolitanism (inspired by the German philosopher Immanuel Kant's *Perpetual Peace*). She is the author of numerous books: *Feminist Contentions: A Philosophical Exchange* (with Judith Butler, Nancy Fraser and Drucilla Cornell; 1994), *The Reluctant Modernism of Hannah Arendt* (2010), *Dignity in Adversity: Human Rights in Troubled Times* (2011) *Exile, Statelessness, and Migration* (2018), and is the recipient of several prestigious awards and lectureships in recognition of her work.

You have been a major voice for many years in scholarly conversations and public debates over how to advance cosmopolitan perspectives in world politics, notably on issues related to transnational migratory flows. In your 2005 Tanner Lectures, Reclaiming Universalism: Negotiating Republican Self-Determination and Cosmopolitan Norms *you sought to reconcile universalist norms with democratic politics, trying to overcome the contradiction between democratic self-determination, which*

*historically evolved in the context of the modern nation state, and
the norms of cosmopolitan justice – a contradiction inscribed in the
UN Charter itself, which affirms both the inalienable sovereignty
of the nation state and the universality of human rights. Today,
we do not appear to be moving collectively towards the latter, we
seem rather in a regression of cosmopolitan possibilities. Given
the rise of exclusionary ethno-nationalism worldwide, how do you
envision the cosmopolitan project, as theory and praxis, going
forward?*

Let me begin by noting how COVID-19, as both reality and
metaphor, can help us think about cosmopolitanism today. As
a result of the pandemic, we have realized that the world has
shrunk in some real way and that we are truly interdependent, and
although nation states have put up barriers and have made travel
and movement more difficult, the reality is that it's a matter of
time before the virus crosses over borders; all nation states can do
is slow its progression, but never completely eliminate it unless
the world has reached a threshold of immunity. No one is safe
until everyone is. This condition is both reality and metaphor: it
is a metaphor for our global interdependence and vulnerability.
What we are experiencing at the current moment, is what I would
call "interdependence without solidarity". There is no solidarity
in the sense that there is no common response that proceeds from
the premise that we share a common fate – being here on the face
of this Earth. This makes me think of Kant when he says: I can go
around the world, but I can't avoid running into someone because
the world is not an infinite open space, but it is like a ball and an
Erdkugel, so we have to learn how to coexist.

However, just because we are interdependent and we realize
this, does not mean, of course, that we also have a cosmopolitan
consciousness, so the objective facts of our human condition, our
shared fate on the face of the earth, does not automatically lead to
a political consciousness of the necessity of exercising solidarity
and coordinating our actions, by trying to live in what one could
can call a world Republic. How to reconcile the aspiration towards
a kind of world Republic, without at the same time giving up on

our right to self-determination, is one of the unresolved tensions of cosmopolitanism. For this reason both Kant and Arendt have seen extreme cosmopolitanism as leading to a kind of despotism. A world state would not be a world Republic, but a form of despotism, so the question remains: how can we think of reconciling cosmopolitan consciousness with our parochial attachments based on our separate aspirations of self-determination? In an age of superpower competition, particularly the fear about world-wide Chinese domination, which could lead to a kind of new Cold War, the cosmopolitan project should try to steer clear both of state-capitalist autocracies like China and weakened liberal democracies like the United States, which are sacrificing democracy for the sake of protectionist capitalist nationalism.

You have been a strong critic of Europe's response to transnational migratory and asylum flows, pointing to the moral failure, the material and symbolic violence of the exclusionary policies that have led the EU to violate foundational human rights conventions and commitments. A fortress Europe system has been designed over the past decades to keep vulnerable populations out, outsourcing their "management" to countries with abysmal human rights records. In the 2000s, Jürgen Habermas and Ulrich Beck, in different ways, envisaged the constitution of an open cosmopolitan Europe acting as an exemplary force in the world. Has that project definitively failed? And if not, what kinds of political and moral resources should be brought to bear on these questions?

I would not say the European project has failed; the answer is more ambivalent. World-wide migratory and asylum flaws have become burning political issues, exploited by populist politicians. But there is also tremendous solidarity among civil society groups that work around migration and asylum issues; so, I find that compared to – let's say the popular consciousness about these issues during the time of the Yugoslav civil war, when I was in Germany as a student in the late 1990s – there is significant mobilization among young people and among activist groups. For me some of the most impressive gestures of cosmopolitan solidarity are undertaken by these activist groups who try to meet asylum boats in the Mediterranean before they are turned back by Libyan coastguards or before they're intercepted by the Italian navy. Organizations like the equivalent of *Médecins sans frontières* undertake such rescue operations at sea, thus raising of awareness among ordinary people for the plight of refugees. It is very easy to be pessimistic about the attitude of governments and institutions, but we should also look at the transformation of popular consciousness. Also, the European Court of Human Rights has taken up issues related to the rights of migrants. In one of the most interesting cases, the case of Hirsi Jamaa (*Hirsi Jamaa and Others v. Italy*), concerning – among other issues – the fate of two asylum seekers who died while being held in Italian custody, the Court recognized the rights of personality of a dead migrant, forbidding that the body could be simply disposed of without any kind of explanation as to what the circumstances were. The very fact that there is now legal recourse because of the stipulations of the European Convention on Human Rights, and the very fact that there is a public discourse about these issues is itself an important step. Does this also mean that Europe can act in exemplary fashion? No, I don't think so: the European Union project has gone from crisis to crisis: the refugee crisis, the Greek financial crisis, etc. but it has still survived as an impressive model of a possible cosmopolitan order, although undoubtedly flawed and with forces within it that are pushing in the other direction.

The major split within the European Union about these migration issues is very visible in the attitude of Hungary, Poland and Croatia, which are blocking migrants entering the EU from the Balkans and refusing to participate in solidarity fees. In the case of Hungary, the European Union has acted in a very cowardly way in that it has not invoked its own principles of the European Charter and the Treaties, sanctioning Hungary for its human rights violations, repressions of civil society and manipulation of the electoral process. I think that the EU should have acted much more censoriously in view of the various violations committed by the Orban government. These compromises around human rights and democratic violations are present within the European Union, so in that sense, the EU is not a shining example, but again I think that total pessimism in this respect would not be correct either.

What is your opinion on the use of the word "populism" today? Its ubiquity is supposed to explain phenomena as diverse as Brexit, Trump, Orban, Bolsonaro etc., or justify the resentments of ordinary people that charismatic politicians manipulate with impossible promises. By using this word indistinctly, aren't we contributing to the ill-naming of things? In referring to leaders, movements and discourses as "populist," are we not saying that what's rational is the cold and instrumental rationality of capitalism, and everything that shows emotion is on the spectrum of populism? Are we thus legitimating the liberal concept which is basically a way of stigmatizing the opponents of liberalism as irrational, foreclosing the possibility of new kinds of politics and new challenges to the status quo? Radical critics of liberal democratic theory such as Chantal Mouffe and Ernesto Laclau, claim that the only inherent connection between right-wing and left-wing populist movements is that both embrace the same fundamental truth about democracy: that it is an ever-shifting contest over how the default "we" of politics is defined. Would you agree with them?

We know that the history of populism is long and, if one goes back to the Roman concept of *il populo*, there are many interesting moments here for learning about building democracy. Machiavelli's political theory of populism is being interpreted as an early moment of democratic resurgence. The 19th century populist movement in the United States of small farmers and businessmen against the monopoly of big banks that were beginning to rob the small farmers of their land, was part of a resistance to the encroachment of big capital. Undoubtedly then, the history of populism, and of course Latin American populism, which is what Laclau has based his theory on, contains many progressive elements. Nevertheless, I think we should be very clear about what contemporary populism is and is not. I don't think that history of populism, whatever emancipatory moments it may contain, should lead us to expect the same about the present populism. As your question suggests it is not just emotional manipulation that is driving contemporary populist movements; it is also a certain disarticulation of the political. This disarticulation is taking place not only through the collapse of party models of representation, but also through the general disregard and skepticism towards representative institutions as such. It is not only political parties that have failed to amalgamate and synthesize people's wishes in different degrees, there is also general skepticism towards representative institutions and representative democracy as such. The feeling is that elites and the technocrats have failed ordinary people. We see this, for example, in the double message of Brexit, accusing the European bureaucracy of having caused material losses in the British countryside, whereas quite to the contrary, the EU was investing a great deal in these areas of Britain by building community centers, swimming pools and the like. So, this disarticulation of the political through the disappearance of the parties, the emergence of a post truth society and decreasing trust in representative institutions, allows for a mobilization of a nostalgia for the past, whether it is Trump and the Make America Great Again movement, whether it is Bolsonaro appealing to a moment in Brazilian history when the pioneers conquered all Brazil and destroyed the forests, or whether it is Erdogan with his nostalgia for Ottoman grandeur. These movements represent a nostalgia for a lost greatness and for the purity of the grand old nation.

In one of your subsequent questions you raise the possibility, justifiably, that this ideology originated with the social and economic turmoil, leading some social classes to become disenfranchised and dislocated. And this is certainly true. Within the United States the success of Trump's mobilization has been able to mobilize the "ressentiment" of the white industrial male worker who has been displaced by the black and brown female post-industrial, service sector worker. Both Democrats and Republicans have participated in the name of globalization in this process. This is why the Democrats have lost the white working class and the trade unions. Biden is a very special phenomenon, precisely because he comes from this class, he was able to recapture Philadelphia,

Wisconsin, Michigan. But I'm not sure that this is what is going on in Erdogan's Turkey or Modi's India. In these countries, a new middle class has emerged, one that is very responsive to these populist and autocratic ideas. They have become affluent with the help of the state and they want to be able to compete at the global level, so they want, on the one hand, to participate in the global neoliberal economy and yet at the same time, their instincts are very authoritarian. So, we have this mixture of market liberalism and authoritarian populism, this is another combination that we have to think about when we talk about contemporary populism.

Students of Carl Schmitt see a necessary conflict between democracy and liberalism. Whereas democracy, they argue, always presupposes a bounded collective subject, a "we" that is distinct from a "they," liberalism is cosmopolitan: it presupposes an unbounded association of individuals entitled to rights. Liberal democracy thus appears as a contradictio in adjecto. *How does this simplistic juxtaposition misrepresent the complexity of contemporary democratic struggles about the boundaries of the demos?*

I think we should not be deceived by the fact that Schmitt interprets democracy as majoritarianism pure and simple. If you go back to his work 1923 *The Crisis of Parliamentary Democracy*, in the final chapters of the book, where he criticizes Rousseau and Marx, he does something very tricky in that he takes Rousseau and Marx, and particularly the young Marx, as representatives of democracy, pure and simple, which he understands as majority rule. And at least in the case of Rousseau, and here I would really want to challenge Schmitt's reading of Rousseau, he attributes to Rousseau the idea of a homogeneous *people*. So, the picture of democracy that emerges from Schmitt's reading is both historically, and theoretically very, very flawed and I frankly don't understand its influence on contemporary thinkers. I think it is because contemporary thinkers on the Left dislike liberalism as much as Schmitt does. But we cannot understand either ancient or modern democracy without looking at its liberal elements in the sense of struggles for rights. Of course, there are other aspects of liberalism such as market freedoms, rule of law, government by discussion etc. which Schmitt emphasizes but here I only want to look at one aspect- the struggle for rights. So, think of the post French-Revolutionary struggles of 1848 and the Paris Commune: these are struggles for equality, equality before the law, to be recognized as a person, but also equality of suffrage, equality of voice. The history of democracy is the history of struggles for equal representation and equal voice by excluded groups, first men who did not own property, the working classes who were not able to vote. Women did not have the right to vote, black and post-colonial people did not have the right to vote, but the point is that the struggles for representation of these groups are part of the history of democracy, you cannot just label them as liberal, they are part of the logic of democracy because democracy is inconceivable without equality. Who are the equals who rule over others, leads us into the question of the boundaries of the demos, but to think that struggles over equality are alien to the project of democracy is just historically and theoretically wrong. In ancient democracies we see the struggles over *isonomia* who has equality in the eyes of the law, *isegoria*, who has the equality to speak, to act, even in the limited and confined understanding of equality and citizenship in the polis. To summarize then: if liberalism is also understood as a struggle for the expansion of human and civil-political rights, which I think it should be, the Schmitt's juxtaposition is simply wrong and misleading.

Fascism tends to arise out of a very specific set of circumstances: when a group of people that once felt politically and economically secure suddenly find themselves feeling marginalized. After World War I, devastating hyperinflation and unemployment exacerbated the humiliation of Germany's defeat, fomenting widespread disillusionment among its citizens. Today the extreme socioeconomic inequality and the disappearing social safety net make people susceptible to fascism's message. Individuals vindictively renounce responsibility for their lives, they define themselves as victims, and soon thereafter as executioners restoring justice. Let us remember that Hitler not only founded his power on the hitherto unpoliticized masses, but was able to secure his legal victory in March of 1933 by mobilizing no less than 5 million former non-voters. Today we are witnessing a discussion about a resurgence of fascism. Is it an appropriate category for analysis or is it historically circumscribed?

The specific features of contemporary populism are: the attack on representative institutions, attack on mainstream media and spreading alternative truths, nostalgia for the past and the like, but there are some elements that are missing in the present if we are to speak of fascism. Even though I am not reluctant to use the term neo-fascism, because I think that there is enough continuity ideologically, we have to be more precise in our concepts. When we look at autocratic leaders like Trump, Bolsonaro, Modi, and we must ask whether they are also claim for themselves the mythical qualities, that let's say Mussolini and Hitler claimed for themselves, and which, the Frankfurt school, notably Adorno and Horkheimer, analyzed so brilliantly in the *Dialectic of Enlightenment*. Adorno and Horkheimer analyzed this phenomenon as the identification with "the little big man," the little person identifies with a figure and projects unto them the mythical qualities they wish to possess. We see this phenomenon in the popularity of Trump and Modi. But all this is not enough to call movements fascist or neo-fascist. Although contemporary commentators do not pay much attention to this, I want to discuss the role of the military in the development of fascist regimes.

Take Latin American cases: populism sometimes mobilized the military, as in the case of Argentina, they were for Perón, but then the military turned against the mobilized masses. What is happening today? Are there paramilitary groups? What games are being played around them? This is extremely important because fascism can only succeed once these institutions are all brought into what in German is called "Gleichschaltung," that is, when they all start walking lockstep. Parliament may not disappear, but Parliament as well as the secret service, the military, the police, etc. are brought into some kind of harmony when they get into lockstep. We cannot really speak of fascism as a system unless, to use Max Weber's language, the monopoly of the means of violence is going to be in the hands of those who want to control the state. And this is a lesson we have to learn from Arendt's analysis of the origins of totalitarianism as well. We do not yet see this with autocratic regimes so far, with the exception of the Myanmar junta and one-party China, Instead, there are attempts to pacify the military, to bribe it so as to remain loyal to the regime.

Let me give you an example from Turkey: the Turkish military was an all-powerful force in the history of the country since the establishment of the Republic in 1923. At the beginning of the millennium in 2000 with the promise of entering the European Union, the Turkish military became "civilianized" and began to lose its power to intervene in the parliamentary process, in the electoral process, which it had done repeatedly in the past. The military was integrated into the neoliberal market. More and more housing was built in military complexes with suburban attractions. The national armament industry was expanded. Without neutralizing the military or without making sure that the monopoly of violence remains in the hands of the state we cannot speak of total fascism. And this is the biggest difference between inter-war years fascism in Europe, and the contemporary situation. In recent weeks in this summer of 2021, we have seen a very interesting clash in the United States between republican senators and representatives and the former military Chief of Staff James Mattis. This man defied the politicians. He openly defied even the President, saying to him that the President cannot tell him, as a military person, to violate his oath of office which is to protect the USA abroad and not to intervene at home. Trump wanted the military to intervene against the *Black Lives Matter* protests and the Chief of Staff who, has resigned since then, refused.. These are details that when we think about fascism, are important to keep in mind.

Throughout her work Hannah Arendt insisted on the separation of the public and private spheres, for which she was often criticized. What can such a strict division between the public and private serve? Is it just a reaction to the times, a provocation, or an aspiration to give stronger grounds to political philosophy?

There are so many dimensions to the concepts of the public and private. First of all, Arendt herself is not sufficiently precise in distinguishing the term public and private. Private in the sense of what concerns the person, the individual, her body, her affective emotional life and the space in which she lives, that is the home, a very important category for Arendt. The second meaning of the private is that which is not public, in the sense of that which is not part of the state and its institutions, here we can think of the economy. Arendt does not have a good theory of the economic or of the market, she basically just accepted some of the old-fashioned sociology from such as the distinction between *Gemeinschaft* and *Gesellschaft*, particularly in *The Human Condition*. Since she also was against economistic reductionism of politics by a certain kind of Marxist logic that saw politics to be just about economic struggles, she stayed away from the economic sphere and did not analyze the interaction between the public and economic aspects of the public and the private. Maybe the third meaning of the private that we can find in Arendt's historical writings, but not in her philosophical writings, is the dimension of civil society and its associations. Here I am thinking of her intervention in the famous debate of school desegregation in Little Rock, Arkansas, when she criticized black parents that were ready to send their children to school, in the protection of federal agents who were following the law in trying to desegregate formerly white schools. All these are different dimensions of this distinction and they need to be reflected upon carefully.

One of the weaknesses of Arendt's political thought is that although as a historian of political events and as a chronicler of events, she of course discusses the subtleties of these issues at the level of meta theory, her political philosophy does not make room for these categorical distinctions. For example, how can we read her analysis of totalitarianism, without distinguishing civil society from the state, from the economy, but when you come to her systematic analysis, particularly in *The Human Condition* these distinctions are not worked out. That's why I always have said that the goal is *thinking with Arendt against Arendt*. Let us learn from her, but let us not be like parrots repeating her, we cannot do that and I don't think she would want us to do' so we have to think about these categories for ourselves, and ask, what may be a sense of privacy that we can retrieve from her. Let me explain with reference to contemporary feminist theory.

There is a debate within contemporary feminist theory about whether concepts like the home and the private sphere are regressive from the standpoint of women, or whether they are helpful to women's causes. The argument that they are regressive says that the home was always also potentially a place of oppression, a place of exclusion and sometimes even a place of danger for women. Some feminist theorists believe that the concept of privacy is unhelpful because it blocks legal and political transformation in these in these spheres. But on the other hand, and I would count myself among them, while other feminists agree about the critique of the potential misuse of privacy to block the gender division of labor and its consequences for women, it is foolish not to want to retrieve and develop a conception of individuality, subjectivity, autonomy from a feminist perspective; all of which Virginia Woolf captured with a beautiful phrase, *a room of one's own*. A room of one's own is the space for women to develop their faculties, the space in which to think, to dream, to imagine. We have to reclaim this aspect of privacy, and I do believe that in her writings, particularly about Rosa Luxemburg and about Rahel Varnhagen, Arendt was very sensitive to this dimension of privacy as individuality, as necessitating a room of one's own in which to flourish.

Finally, last year you joined the international call for support of the Institute for Philosophy and Social Theory in Belgrade, which fought (ultimately successfully) for the preservation of its academic autonomy. Do you believe that intellectuals can make a difference and, if so, what kind?

Institutions of free thinking, institutions of oppositional thinking are nowadays under siege in many countries of the world. We have to fight to preserve these spaces. The reach of the state, and the reach of the technocracy is so powerful that the present danger is not only immediate repressive intervention, firing of faculty, jailing of students such as we see in Erdogan's intervention in the Bosphorus University in Istanbul or with China's crackdown upon the opposition and the media in Hong Kong. There are also more subtle forms, through which institutions of free thinking and philosophy are being technocratized and transformed into institutions of applied science or artificial intelligence. And here I don't mean to say anything against the pursuit of science; we've had enough anti-science nonsense during the COVID pandemic, with the spread of anti-vaccine, counter enlightenment views. That's not my point; rather, I want to emphasize that there is also the struggle of technocracy against philosophy and against humanistic thinking because such thinking is neither subservient to the market, nor to the state and nor to the military-industrial complex. To maintain such thinking alive by preserving academic autonomy is extremely important and valuable.

Interview conducted by Zona Zarić

HOW TO OVERCOME RESENTMENT
Cynthia Fleury

Cynthia Fleury is a French philosopher and psychoanalyst, Professor of the Humanities and holder of the Health Chair at the National Conservatory of Arts and Crafts and Associate Professor at the Ecole nationale supérieure des mines de Paris (Mines-ParisTech). She also heads department of philosophy at the Sainte-Anne Hôpital (psychiatry and neurosciences). She previously taught at the American University of Paris and was a researcher at the National museum of Natural history, as well as the youngest member of the National Ethics Committee. This year she was awarded the Legion of Honour for her work on care in the public sphere. Author of numerous books: *Les Pathologies de la démocratie* (2005), *La Fin du courage : la reconquête d'une vertu démocratique* (2010), *Les Irremplaçables* (2015), *Le soin est un humanisme* (2019), Métaphysique de l'imagination (2020), *Ci-gît l'amer, guérir du ressentiment* (2020). She defines our times as a time of loss of political, moral and individual courage, since there is no political courage without moral courage in a society based on merciless economic struggle, resulting in dysfunctional individuals and collectives.

Our quotidian has become calmer, centered around comfort, consumerism, we have become incapable of projecting into the future, softened by comfort, we have thus forgotten that we are really mortal, vulnerable, exposed, psychologically and physically fragile. Daily life makes it difficult to think togetherness, both the trivial and what unites us. Has our tolerance to risk and uncertainty been diminished? What remains of illusory fantasies about the Anthropocene since the outbreak of the pandemic?

2020 will be the beginning of the new millennium, specifically the twenty-first century. Chronologically, of course, the date is off, but on the level of experience, but also in an epistemological and paradigmatic sense, 2020 is when we collectively felt the crash of the system, had the experience of breakdown. Scientific literature in the humanities has for a number of years been using terms like "Anthropocene" and "systemic risk," and have been working out "scenarios of breakdown." However, what remains "unpublished," is the experience of having lived through this theorization, in the North, by Western countries, specifically by the financially best protected individuals in urban systems. In 2020, we have experienced in our lives, on our own skin, in a rather banal, ordinary manner, a certain degree of restrictions, interruptions, constraints, false starts. We know now that this was no mere crisis, but rather a recurring phenomenon, which forces us to develop thinking and protocols of resilience and homeostasis. The use of metaphors from medicine is not insignificant, because societies and individuals must now invent a new way of life, which demands adaptation and not over-adaptation, for we know very well that the latter causes burn-out and other mental issues. We fantasized about the impending breakdown, or else denied it, yet we have not yet "lived" it in its "reality." We are entering a world of depleted resources and unequal access to them. And a world in which social contracts are increasingly destabilized by economies and politics of survival, exception, emergency, of priority triage.

The Diagnostic and Statistical Manual of Mental Disorders (DSM-5), the reference book for psychiatrists, indicates that a person who feels they have been a victim often feels they have the right to be violent. In your latest book, Here Lies Bitterness: Healing from Resentment (2022), you try to explain violence as the organization and symbolization of the process of conflictuality. You go so far as to say that the role of politics is sublimation. What does that mean for us today, given that the dominant ideologies seem to be burning bridges rather than opening up directions?

In the book, I tried to explain that we conflate all too easily politics and violence, politics and the move to action, even if politics is on the side of theory of action, and not the side of action, of overflow. In fact, politics is more about the sublimation of violence and developing protocols of conflictuality than violence as such, violence that has no end other than itself. Politics is structurally a process of sublimation, in the sense that it "differs," it, of course, makes decisions about the present time, but its ultimate aim is to create a future, viable, durable time. We live in technical, "instantaneous" worlds, depoliticized, overly emotional, in which frustration is delegitimized, even though it contains certain structural qualities for a person or society. In my book I take up the infamous quotation from Freud that concerns the three impossible professions – psychoanalysis, education, governance – considering them as one and the same, or as the first two were perhaps the condition of possibility of the last. We continue to lie to ourselves about the question of good governance by restricting this question to political governance in the sense of executive machine of political power, a set of people around the president and the ministerial cabinet; yet the question of good governance is much broader than mere execution of a presidential mandate. The question is to be found further down the line, in education and care. There are a number of us working to elaborate this question of good governance, to think the conditions of its legitimation and efficiency precisely through education and care for individuals – the very individuals who elect the to the government, in the narrower and representative sense.

What is the difference between individualism, de Tocqueville's democratic egoism, and individuation?

Egoism is "a passionate and exaggerated love for oneself," says Tocqueville, "which brings a man back only to himself and to prefer himself to anything else." Individualism on the other hand is a "thoughtful and calm feeling." In defining these notions in this way, Tocqueville puts himself in the liberal tradition of methodological individualism, which held up this idea along with a concept of negative freedom. And while I also am an inheritor of methodological individualism, modern societies have put into place a more zealous individualism, less inclined towards so-called positive freedom, or towards public responsibility and any kind of disinterested engagement. Here we have a difference between individualism and individuation: the former designates a process of subjectivation that forgets everything it owes to collective structures in constituting itself, while the latter is cognizant of this process and cares to enough to preserve its collective mentality. In *Les irremplaçable*, I tried to show how the preservation of democracy in the sense of the social legal state depended on the kind of principle used to individuate individuals. "We are not replaceable." I wrote at the time, "The rule of law is nothing without the irreplaceability of individuals." The trick here is to understand how the much-maligned individual actually protects democracy from its entropic tendencies. Do we need to rethink anew what means the "individual?" In fact, it is the kind of process of subjectivation, individuation without individualism, that guarantees the duration of democracy. Democracy has often been studied as a political system and the society that accompanied the emergence of free subjects. It is important to understand how the individual can themselves work towards the lasting of democracy.

An idea recurs across several of your works, such as La Fin du courage and also more recently in Les Irremplaçables – a true theory of the subject. It was described well by Vladimir Jankélévitch as "that thing that needs to be done, it is I who must do it." How does philosophy permit us to ground a theory of courage that articulates the individual and the collective? A theory which, as you say, "calls to create the whole, even though we are only one part?"

I have been working for a long time on the dysfunctionality of democracy and regulatory tools to mitigate the gap between principles and effective practice. This kind of work includes institutional reform, but also behavioral change of citizens, which means the kind of regulatory tools individuals have access to. In this vein, I have proposed the following hypothesis: might we consider courage a democratic virtue, necessary for allowing democracy to last and protect itself from dysfunction? Ultimately, I have chosen to examine courage, since I had a straightforward intuition. Democracy of the old type presents grand illusions that lapse into automatism or the status quo. As if democracy functioned all of its own accord, in an autonomous way, without having to fight for it. As if democracy were so strong that there was no need to do anything. In fact, democracy is always one side that confronts another. Democracy is not the place where rights just lie about, rather it is a space where rights could exist. But to obtain those rights, it is necessary to struggle. For me, the crucial point is to deconstruct this illusion of automatic nature within democracy. Courage is that virtue citizens need in order to fight against the anti-democratic onslaught. On an individual level, courage is a motivating factor, an operational virtue, which puts into action. It is a cardinal virtue rendering operational all other virtues. Vladimir Jankélévitch states that courage is the virtue of initiation, calling it "the inaugural threshold of a decision." In *La volonté de vouloir*, he points out that one must will the will. You are aware of course of the phrase "where there is a will, there is a way:" when I was a child, I did not understand it, until the day I learned that the obstacle does not lie in the domain of 'might', but rather in will. To will something is where the difficulty lies. Once this has been overcome, the rest comes more easily, even if the process is conducted bit by bit, in a year or twenty. Courage is then an inchoative virtue, which is to say it is related to beginnings. Nevertheless, is it enough to will to be courageous? Of course not. Vladimir Jankélévitch tells us that we also need to stop delegating and accept what each one must do. Only then does "one" become "I," – master of my situation, independent agent. The philosopher avers that courage is a dispersed sowing, a fertility by randomness. On this point, he often asked me whether it was history that produced courage or the other way round. Really, the two are married together, in a strong dialectic. For the philosopher, however, courage is simply ethics. Initially, ethics of courage existed only in an individual sense. Just because I am courageous does not mean you are too; there is no *mimesis* of courage. And yet, paradoxically, in the long run, ethics of courage emerges only from the collective. This brings up the following questions: how is collective emulation produced? How is courage transmitted? How is it learned? Enabling the emergence of collective courage around oneself, starting from individual courage, this is one of the most difficult processes to put into practice. Courage is victory-less. It is a beginning – but then also a beginning ever anew. One must always return to the struggle. What is more, success does not decree the truth of courage: a courageous act is such in itself, regardless of success. It is possible to be courageous without winning. On the other hand, it also lasts long-term, which means it becomes a question of Pascal's wager. Long-term studies have shown that courage saves being – literally. In short, the process of putting courage into practice includes several temporalities that have to combine together.

The cult of the beautiful body, beautiful image, of purity – are these inimical to psychoanalytic culture and the idea of the unconscious?

Being affected by the beauty of a body is not at all inimical to psychoanalysis, but I realize this is not the issue. Rather, the issue is alienation from one's own image, fantasy, idealization, being a prisoner of mimetic rivalry, social codes of beauty and behavior – now, this, yes, this is inimical to analytic work, to critique. The latter consist precisely in overcoming all forms of alienation or normalization of reification. The idea of the absolute or of purity is equally dangerous, as it carries with it an inflexibility, a psychological rigidity. The radicalization of mind and one's actions goes along with dichotomous thinking, rejection of complexity, authoritarian ascribing of "purity" and "impurity." The unconscious is a language where everything can coexist, without any discord. It is not a happy coexistence, but rather a combination of previous and current ways of being, a mixing of times and spaces. The unconscious is very flexible.

Is the principle of universal basic income contrary to our entire history, our morality and culture?

Universal basic income is a new chapter in the social history of emancipatory forms from systems of bare survival. In other words, labor should be emancipatory, allowing the worker to produce their own ends and give them the feeling of possibility to transform the world, to an extent. Once again, we are in a position in which work is felt to be alienated, stripped of meaning, and which renders less secure and more precarious, to boot.

Today we see the return of the debate counterposing security and freedom, flaring up during the health crisis as well as at moments of terrorist attacks. Our societies seem to be animated by these drives, sublimation appears to be on the wane, to the advantage of denial and taking action. These drives seem to be taking over in a world that has no way to limit them. Immediacy, speed, intensity, fluidity call forth a society without frustration or delay. Yet, in the public sphere (the news, entertainment), post-industrial and post-traumatic societies after World War II do not seem like they are "sublimating" much. Anything that delays immediate satisfaction is seen as an obstacle. Frustration is no longer allowed. Will this last? Is it reversible? What is the link between this and the politics of disengagement, short-termist and dissociative as it is?

My interest in disengagement comes from studying Wilhelm Reich and the production of collective resentment. To be properly understood, we need to return to Reich's *Mass Psychology of Fascism* (1933), in which he inverts the traditional narrative of a great leader at the head of a crowd or those reasons ascribed to a stick figure version of Hegel (although for him, the cunning of reason is indeed an attempt to use the idea of a great man and wild passion, to bring about a complex dialectic between the event and the great individual, thus animating History). Reich is interesting because he takes seriously the responsibility of the masses, hidden behind a veil of "disengagement." In this way, we understand a little better, how, little by little, in a latent and irreversible way, individuals form a corps linked mutually together only by resentment; and then how this wretched and deformed corps will deliberately identify a "leader" allowing the authorization of a deadly drive, releasing the tensions that have been ruminating and gnawing at it for a long time. This "other" needs to be selected, perhaps even elected, to allow to show openly what has long been feared because it is so ugly. "Hitler not only based his power originally on masses which previously had been essentially unpolitical; he also achieved his final victory in March, 1933, in a "legal" manner, by the mobilization of not less than five million of previous non-voters, that is, unpolitical people." And Reich shows that this reclaimed disengagement was never any kind of "neutrality" or "indifference;" rather, it was a latency, dissimulation of personal resentment, waiting for its moment (without overt consciousness of this patience – hence the rumination), which waiting deepened its malaise and then also increased the strength of its action, and which willingly – consciously or not – removed personal responsibility. The "mass" is born that day and moment when all the subjects forming it abandon their subjectivity, renouncing with impunity responsibility for their lives, seeing themselves as victims turned executioners reestablishing justice.

You have been active in numerous social movements for democracy and freedom. Recent among these struggles was that of the Institute for Philosophy and Social Theory in Serbia, for which you joined an international appeal of support and which yielded positive results. Do you think that intellectuals can make a difference in society and if so, what kind? What, in your opinion, is the role and place of intellectuals in contemporary societies and social struggles?

The role of intellectuals is decisive in defending non-authoritarian regimes: they are the ones who bring this essential, deliberative power of critique, this regulation by way of *logos*, which is so characteristic of democracies, and which individuals need to maintain the qualitative process of subjectivization. Their role is also to differentiate the system of the Real, of anything that could appear here and now or in the future, from the most foreclosed system of social reality, for now. They deconstruct the illusions of the socio-historical order, system of domination and reification.

Interview conducted by Zona Zarić

"THE WAR ON MIGRATION" AS A SEQUEL TO "THE WAR ON TERROR"
Étienne Balibar

Étienne Balibar is Professor Emeritus at University of Paris X – Nanterre (2002), Professor at University of California Irvine (2020), and the Center for modern European philosophy at Kingston University. A member of the *Parti communiste français* since 1961, he was expelled in 1981 for criticizing the party's policy on immigration. Co-author of *Reading Capital* with Louis Althusser, author of *The Nation Form: History and Ideology, Race, Nation, Class: Ambiguous Identities*, with Immanuel Wallerstein, *Masses, Classes, Ideas: Studies on Politics and Philosophy Before and After Marx, Secularism and Cosmopolitanism: Critical Hypotheses on Religion and Politics, Spinoza, the Transindividual*. He is the 2020 laureate of the *Miladin Životić* Award for Critical Engagement, conferred by the Institute for Philosophy and Social Theory of the University of Belgrade.

Let us begin with the issue of commitment: the term has different meanings in different languages. You speak of commitment in the Pascalian and Sartrean sense. What inspires this idea of engagement in your own experiences and your own philosophical references?

It was Sartre who reused Pascal's vocabulary in what is considered to be the "founding" text of his theory of engagement (the 1945 "Presentation of Modern Times"), citing the famous formula: "you are embarked" (vous êtes embarqués). This initiates a dialectic of opposites: you have to choose (wager; *il faut parier*), but in a situation that you do not choose. I think that the Pascal reference is fundamental, because it shows that with commitment, it is not a simple decision of choosing between one way of life or work or another, but rather of what determines all life and all thought. It is therefore a question of transforming contingency into necessity. But the Pascal reference suggests that what is at stake there is redemption or damnation in a future life (a "beyond"), whereas it is the meaning of the present life, or what Marx called "the here below" (*Diesseitigkeit*). This raises the question of the consequences of commitment, which I think is the fundamental question. What do we do about the errors that commitment inevitably entails? From a Sartrean point of view, which is that of a freedom that is always "transcendent", one can "free oneself" and sometimes this is what one must do. I think that the higher form of commitment consists in 'obstinacy' (as Negt and Kluge say in History and Obstinacy), which does not mean blindly defending the same mistakes, but seeking the means to understand and rectify them for oneself and especially for the 'we' to which a commitment binds you. For commitment means to get outside of oneself. This is what I have tried to do in my dealings with the communist commitment – without being certain of having succeeded, of course.

The idea of the end, or at least the decline of intellectuals, is defended in a significant number of theoretical texts published over the last thirty years. Do you agree with this thesis and what is, in your opinion, the role and place of the commitment of intellectuals in contemporary societies and in social struggles?

This question is meaningless without an investigation into and an effort to define what "intellectuals" mean. Two ideas seem to me to be important in this respect in the tradition to which I belong. On the one hand, that of Marx, who included the "division of manual and intellectual labour" among the great structures of domination throughout history, even if its modalities are constantly changing. On the other hand, that of Gramsci, who makes "intellectuals" (or at least some of them, with an "organic" capacity for intervention in social struggles) the builders of hegemony, power relations and subordination (or counter-powers defying the established order), but who also affirm the existence of an "intellectual function" that goes beyond the dominant institutional intellectuality and can be assumed by individuals from all social classes, particularly through their activism. Today's 'globalised' capitalist society (which I call with others a society of 'absolute capitalism') is completely transforming the facts of this problem, using the resources of new technologies and communication by shifting the locus of real power in society. In fact, it no longer needs intellectuals in the "bourgeois" sense of the term (which includes academics, "independent" artists, even scholars dedicated to "pure" research, etc.). It is a non-bourgeois or post-bourgeois capitalist society. Hence, it is a paradoxical and perilous situation at the same time: intellectuals who want to be "critical" (the "traitors" to the existing order, as Marx said) must also, and perhaps first of all, defend their right to exist and the institutions that allow them to work. But they have no chance of doing so if they stick to a backward-looking definition of the intellectual (even if "committed") and take a defensive position. The articulation with social struggles (which doesn't mean only class struggle, but ecology, feminism, anti-racism and decolonialism, etc.) is therefore both an ethical-political choice and a way of bringing the "intellectual function" to life in society.

In June 1970, your teacher and someone who fundamentally influenced your thought, Louis Althusser, published one of his masterly texts in the journal La Pensée, *entitled "Ideology and Ideological Apparatus of the State." In this text, the philosopher distinguishes between two state apparatuses: the repressive apparatus and the ideological apparatus of the state. The latter is less visible and is composed of all the institutions whose ideology it transmitted to the to the whole of society by the classes that run the state. What is the difference between the ideological apparatus of the state of the 1970s of which Althusser spoke and the ideological apparatus of the state today?*

That would be a very long discussion... I learned a lot from Althusser, both through his texts and in the form of a long friendship and personal collaboration. I am very happy to observe that some of his texts, often incomplete and aporetic, because they were elaborated under conditions of great personal and collective tension, continue to make people think or even act today. The opposition between "repressive apparatuses" and "ideological apparatuses," which has often been criticized (notably by Foucault), shouldn't be understood in a typological way (even if Althusser indulges in classifying large institutions into one or the other category) but rather in a dynamic or strategic way, as a sign of the fact that power relations oscillate between two poles and combine them in unequal proportions. But the most delicate and potentially the most fruitful problem concerns the reference made here to the state. This is obviously inherited from the notion of *indirecta postestas*, which belongs to the tradition of political theology (Bellarmin, Hobbes) and which in the 19th century led to the concept of 'spiritual power' in Auguste Comte. By combining it with the Marxist idea of "the dominant ideology as the ideology of the ruling class," Althusser is able to take up the Gramscian program of an "enlargement of the concept of the state" which places the state in an occult way in the unconscious infrastructure of individual subjectivity itself.

But one may wonder whether this structural construction is still adequate (at least without variation) to the way in which subjectivities are formatted in current capitalism (which from this point of view is well characterized as 'neo-liberalism'). A young Greek philosopher, Maria Kakogianni, proposed the concept of 'ideological market apparatuses' to record the novelty of the mechanisms of interpellation of individuals as 'subjects' in a society where ideological domination happens not so much through the imaginary of sovereignty as through that of competition and profitability to which one must 'adapt' (Barbara Stiegler). I'm tempted to think that we have here another indication of the emergence of a capitalism without bourgeoisie in the classical sense. It is clear from the current crisis engendered by the Covid-19 pandemic, a crisis whose moral dimensions are as fundamental as the economic ones, that collective confusion and even despair result as much, if not more, from the feeling of the failure of the market than from the feeling of the failure of the state... Or rather the state is part of it, because states today are being instrumentalized by the market to a degree that is unprecedented.

At the time when the Yellow Vests movement was at its zenith, you said that through this movement – which presents many contradictions – one notices the process where "the excluded include themselves". How do you see this movement in the context of new class struggles in France?

As a "movement" which is not organized but individualized, the Yellow Vests have probably completed their trajectory. But the revolt against the effects of exclusion (deprivation of active citizenship at the same time as deprivation of recognition and social protection) of which it was an expression is not going to disappear. On the contrary, it may be thought that the extraordinarily unequal and authoritarian conditions in which society's efforts to control the pandemic (which itself affects individuals and social groups in an extraordinarily unequal way, deepening what I have called the "anthropological differences," that is, the differences that fracture the human species as such) are major new insurrectionary phenomena. But the question of what political direction they will take will be raised in an acute way. In the Yellow Vests movement, wherein many thought they could read a French form of the "populism" that was also developing elsewhere at the same time (think of Trump, Bolsonaro, etc.), it is remarkable that xenophobic and authoritarian tendencies were marginalized and eventually overcome by the participants themselves. There is no guarantee that this will always be the case. Insurgencies are the driving force behind political change in the world today, but ambivalence is their fundamental characteristic, and therefore the political problem they face.

The last chapter of your latest book, Histoire interminable: d'un siècle l'autre, (Ecrits I), *is a strategic plea for a socialist project for the 21ˢᵗ century. If previous socialisms – those that materialized in the National Social State as you call it – thought politics in terms of pure power relations, what is the interpretative framework of the policy you propose for 21ˢᵗ century socialism?*

In this final chapter of my book, I take care to underline the hypothetical nature of the descriptions and proposals that I put forward. All this is a matter for discussion and therefore an object of reflection. I have taken the risk of using a broad and even extremely broad (I have been reproached) concept of "socialism." In it I turned Friedrich von Hayek's thesis, which opposed liberalism as absolute market deregulation to all forms of state intervention in the economy, against itself; and I have included both the authoritarian and single-party planning models of "real socialism" as well as the social democratic formations of Western Europe and the United States (thus the New Deal), and the "development" policies of the Third World. In particular, it was a question of inscribing all these policies and the corresponding institutional innovations in the history of class struggles, to underline (after Keynes and Negri) the decisive function of the Russian Revolution of 1917 which inspired in capitalism the sense of urgency of social policies (which it has lost today...), and to understand that the capitalism in which we live today is not, according to the classic formula, an "antechamber of socialism," but a postsocialist regime, which was built by deconstructing socialism in its different forms.

I also stressed, as you recall, that these socialist experiences (very heterogeneous) have the common feature of having dealt with the social question in a national framework, which is also a result of their statism and explains the difficulty of rethinking the question of social transformation in a transnational way, by mobilizing the corresponding forces at this scale. Yet this is what is required by both the more or less reversible effects of "globalization" and the decidedly irreversible effects of the ecological disaster. A "socialism" of the 21st century (I have put the term in scare quotes, to show that it isn't necessarily the best or the definitive term) should combine, in an open manner, objectives and forms of political action that are very heterogeneous and on very different scales: I have said, hypothetically international regulations (of labor, finance, environmental standards, armaments...), utopias (i.e. small- or large-scale experiments in new ways of living together, therefore of consumption, property, etc.), and finally insurrections (in the broadest sense, preferably non-violent at that).

Last June, you co-signed an appeal alerting the public sphere to the fact that Emmanuel Macron is not fighting against racism, but against anti-racism in France. How do you see Emmanuel Macron's presidency as a whole? Is there something fundamentally new that he has brought to French political life compared to his predecessors? And how do you feel knowing that the French president has indicated that he was "very inspired" by your work and even wanted to do his thesis with you?

I think these statements by the then candidate Emmanuel Macron were part of a communication campaign, as were his even more insistent references to working with Paul Ricoeur. But after all, I have no reason and no way of determining the degree of his sincerity. So, I have nothing more to say on this. As for the combination in the discourse and action of a French political leader of modernizing and reforming rhetoric, possibly including a social component, with an instrumentalization of the xenophobic and, in fact, racist theme of 'French identity', it is absolutely nothing new. What is very worrying is that the President is making this shift to the right, and even to the extreme right (he is not the only one in French politics, but he is in power) at a time when a whole series of factors (including terrorism) may push public opinion towards an "active" form of institutional racism. This is the phenomenon which, a few years ago, I called "the impotence of the almighty," one of the matrices of fascism in European history.

Three years ago, in an article in Le Monde, you wrote that the European Union, threatened by technocratic authoritarianism and the rise of neo-fascism, was in danger of exploding. In that article, you called for a historical refoundation of Europe based on a new type of federation. In the meantime, the situation is only getting visibly worse. In your opinion, what is the most likely solution for the EU in the current situation: dissolution or re-foundation? And, can it be said that the destruction of former Yugoslavia can be seen as an indicator of Europe's inability to face its own destiny?

My answer – forgive the evasion – is that I don't know. The destruction of Yugoslavia (I never use the expression "ex-

Yugoslavia"...) is of course, among other things (because there are also internal causes, but we are here by definition in a topology where the internal and external constantly exchange places) a mark of this incapacity of Europe that you evoke. But there are many others. Brexit is another, of course, and above all the criminal management of the issue of migrants and refugees in the Mediterranean, before, during and after Merkel's initiative in 2015 (whose sabotage was carried out jointly by Hungary and France). Some commentators welcomed the European Commission's "recovery" program (including a very limited debt pooling component) in the face of the current crisis as a "Hamiltonian moment" – therefore federalist – for Europe. Let's admit the comparison, although it covers all sorts of difficulties as to the nature of state construction in America in the 18th century and in Europe in the 21st century... In fact, nothing is at stake because, on the one hand, the question now being asked is what is a currency in the world of generalized indebtedness (or, in which monetary regime will Europe have to commit itself, given the international balance of power); and, on the other hand, the possibility of managing a common budget without enhanced democratic legitimacy for the European institutions is more dubious than ever (and this legitimacy is almost non-existent). So, we are left with the situation I have described: there will be no policy for the peoples of Europe if European federalism does not reinvent itself (let us think of what we said above about regulations). But the opponents of this federalism (for reasons that are often opposed to each other, but whose negativity is combined) have all the means to block it. I don't have the means to say anything else. Like others, I am thinking of 'Sleepwalkers' (in the sense of Hermann Broch, since taken up again).

In a lecture you gave in October 2018 in Montreal, you said that after the "war on terror," we are now talking about the "war on migration." We can see that the issue of migration deepens the divide not only between the left and the right, but also within the left itself, between those who advocate a so-called security solution and those who advocate the humanitarian position. You yourself support the thesis that the right to movement and hospitality are fundamental rights. How do you think the issue of migration should be understood in the context of contemporary capitalism and what is the appropriate strategy for a progressive left on this issue?

As I cannot sum up all my arguments in a few words, as they are moreover constantly evolving, except on the core point which is the recognition of the political and moral centrality of this question, I will content myself with three remarks.

First, we must cease isolating ourselves within this dichotomy of "security" and "humanitarian," which is itself a component of the rhetoric of war against migration, or rather against migrants and refugees – which taken together I call the "wanderers" (les errants). The reception of wanderers in "human" conditions, that is, in accordance with international law, may pose problems of policing like any movement of peoples in exceptional situations. But it does not constitute a danger to the "security" of European countries or their communities. Its amalgamation with the issue of 'terror' is purely and simply racist (especially through its Islamophobic component). Second, the analysis of international migration in today's world, with all the complexity of the concrete determinations that accompany it (orientation of migration from South to South, from South to North, the combination of legal and illegal forms; the correlation, or not, with the transformation of the international division of labor, etc.) is not a simple matter. Rosa Luxemburg (and her successors, analyzing the "world-system" of historical capitalism) rethought it as an articulation between the capitalist "centers" and their "peripheries." Today the centers are in Europe or America, but also in China, in South-East Asia, in the Persian Gulf... and the "peripheries" from where proletarianized overpopulation arises.

Finally third, the regulation of population movements and above all the recognition of the "right to rights" (Arendt) for all categories of human beings on the surface of the earth, territorialized and deterritorialized, nationalized and denationalized, is the heart of a new cosmopolitan law and a new international order, to which all the conservative forces (including those on the 'left' here and there in the world) are opposed, but which are inevitably being put on the agenda by the entry of humanity into the age of climatic and demographic upheavals (to which we now see that health upheavals will now be added). I don't know how long it will take for the majority of our peoples to become aware of this, nor what kind of violence will be the condition for this (I do not believe, unfortunately, that it will exclude genocidal practices); nor, a fortiori, [how long it will take] for governments and international institutions to take charge of the problem. But I don't see how this can be avoided.

Interview conducted by Zona Zarić and Ivica Mladenović

THE PANDEMIC AND NEW CHALLENGES FOR DEMOCRACY
Wolfgang Merkel

Wolfgang Merkel is a political scientist who influenced global debates on authorities and democracy. He is director of the "Democracy and Democratisation" research program at the Social Science Research Centre Berlin (WZB) and professor of Political Science at the Humboldt University Berlin. He is a member of a number of key bodies, including the prestigious Berlin-Brandenburg Academy of Sciences and Humanities. He is also a non-party member of the Basic Values Commission of the Executive Committee of the German Social Democratic Party (SPD). His latest work focuses on the crisis of democracy and consequences of globalization on societies. His recent book publications include *The Struggle over borders. Cosmopolitanism and Communitarianism* (ed., 2019 Cambridge University Press; with de Wilde, Koopmans, Merkel, Strijbis, Zürn); *Democracy and Crisis. Challenges in Turbulent Times* (ed., 2018 with Sascha Kneip, Springer); *Handbook of Political, Social, and Economic Transformation* (ed. with Raij Kollmorgen and Hans-Jürgen Wagener 2018 Oxford University Press); *The Future of Representative Democracy* (2011, Cambridge University Press, together with Sonia Alonso and John Keane).

In a recent article, you claim that democracies have rarely disappeared via armed coups in the last 50 years; instead, they have eroded and died slow deaths. Many consolidated, or, as you would say embedded democracies are facing attempts to capture the state or at least to ensure dominant role of the executive power. Are we witness to the global death throws of democracy?

No, we aren't. But the democratic euphoria of the 1990s is over. After 2000, a decade of democratic stagnation followed. It ended the third wave of democratization. The challenge to democracy and a slow but almost global decline of democratic quality has begun and continues to today. It affected even Europe when right-wing populist parties resembled and stimulated nationalist and chauvinist protest against the liberal and cosmopolitan elements of democratic rule. However, there is no doubt that the young democracies in Eastern Europe declined much faster than among the well-established democracies in Western Europe. Poland has become a defective democracy, Hungary and Serbia are at the threshold of authoritarian rule, while Russia or Belorussia are already open autocratic regimes or always had been since the collapse of communism.

The global pandemic goes hand in hand with the massive restriction of the human rights. This is apparently widely (mis) used in the states that are backsliding in democratic order, Serbia more than others, it would seem. At this point we still do not see the end of the pandemic. How do you perceive this coalition between (populist) authoritarianism and securitization based on anti-virus measures?

The pandemic turned out to be a new and hitherto unknown challenge to all democracies. This is true for Denmark, France, and Germany. Even in those high-quality democracies, fundamental rights were suspended. It was the moment of executive power. It resembled more the ideas of the right constitutionalist Carl Schmitt than the liberal values of John Rawls or Ralf Dahrendorf. The ruling strongmen of already defective democracies such as Hungary, Serbia, or Turkey used the pandemic largely uncontrolled or supported by "their" parliamentary majorities to further autocratize their countries. If there will be a severe second COVID-19 infection wave, it could mean the final coup de grace for those moribund hybrid regimes. Securitization in times of Corona can be an authoritarian threat to democracy (Hungary, Serbia) but it can be also democratically organized such as in Denmark or Sweden.

We live in a decade of protest politics, Black Lives Matter protests being only the most recent among them. Serbia is just in the middle of newest wave of protests, with brutal police reaction. How do you see the potential of protest & social movements having in mind rise of the right-wing and conservative forces everywhere?

Our times are characterized by the simultaneity of culturally progressive movements such as "Black Lives Matter" or "Fridays for Future" and reactionary nationalist and intolerant xenophobic rightist protest movements. Some of them seem to be partially orchestrated from above as in Serbia and Turkey, but many are also emerging self-organized by certain, mostly lower, segments of West European Societies. That is what we can call the dark side of civil society. Moreover, the simultaneous co-existence of progressive and regressive-authoritarian protest movements demonstrate the deeply divided societies in Europe, North- and South America. To put is schematically: on the one, the rightist side we find lower middle-class globalization losers and on the other side the cosmopolitan winners of globalization. The socio-economic cleavage intersects with the cultural one; this makes the conflicts so complex and normatively confusing.

German chancellor and French president have been supportive of the Serbian President, Aleksandar Vučić in the name of stabilocracy in the region, contributing to strengthening his power and capturing the institutions in Serbia. We are now facing collapse of institutions, especially the health system due to long-term negligence. What is the responsibility of the European leaders in this disintegration of the democratic institutions, all in the name of keeping stability in the region? Is stability really possible without democratic institutions?

Unfortunately, yes. Autocracies can be rather stable. Look at China, North Korea, Belorussia, or even Saudi Arabia. The US but also the EU mostly gave a preference to stability before human rights and democracy. Henry Kissinger once said related to the Chilean dictator Augusto Pinochet: "It does not matter whether he is a bastard, but whether he is our bastard." The EU, President Macron or Chancellor Merkel are not that outspoken like Henry Kissinger during the cold war, but secretly they too often follow the same slogan. But to be honest: it was not only Merkel in Germany who perceived Vučić at the beginning of his term as hope for stable democracy. This wrong perception is now waning. The brutal repression of the protests (or the orchestration of them) is now strongly changing the once positive perception of Vucic in Germany. Autocratic stability however, in a society with strong democratic and civil forces such as in Serbia is highly improbable already in the medium run.

We have seen a substantial rise of the Green Party with weakening of the both social-democrats and Die Linke. At the same time AfD also managed to grow its constituency. Is green the new left? How do you evaluate their program? What is wrong with left forces, why do they fail to win the trust of citizens?

The Greens are the "new cultural left." In socio-economic terms, it is the "new middle" supported by the professionally well-educated and economically well-off people. The Greens benefit from the emerging cleavage between cosmopolitans and communitarians. They represent the modern cosmopolitanism, beyond left and right. Both Greens and AFD are heavily profiting from the continuing decline of social democracy (SPD). The former social democratic voters of the new middle class and the traditional workers have left the SPD. The middle-class voters turned to the Greens and many of the traditional blue-collar workers opted for the nationalist AFD. The next government in Germany will probably be formed by a CDU/CSU – Green coalition.

The campaign of the right-wing ruling party in Croatia has been supported officially by prominent European politicians, among whom Ursula von der Leyen, current President of the European Commission, which drew heavy criticism and reactions that codes of conduct have been broken. What is your reaction to this interference in the national elections? Is impartiality an illusion to be overcome?

Impartiality in politics is indeed an illusion and may be not a very progressive one. We have to understand politics better in terms of interests, power, and values. Was the EU impartial during the Euro-crisis? Of course not. The economic interests of the north, particularly of Germany, inspired the wrong austerity policy against the European south. The direct interference into policy making against the electorally legitimized national governments was highly problematic. Interference into national elections however, is not automatically undemocratic. For example: would it not be an interesting innovation if the world's citizen have a right to vote in US-elections since they are heavily affected by the decisions of US-governments. I would favor some kind of "interference" into the Hungarian, Polish, or Serbian elections supporting the democratic forces against the autocratization of their countries. The principle of non-interference is to some extent a relic of the national past in a globalized world. It helps autocrats more (Chinese model) than democratic forces.

Finally, you have joined the international call to support the Serbian Institute for Philosophy and Social Theory, which brought some positive results. Do you believe that intellectuals can make a difference today, and if so, what kind?

In general, I am skeptical about the power of intellectuals to influence politics. But there are situations where such a broad national and international alliance of intellectuals can shape public discourse. And if intellectuals have good access to the media and links to popular strata they might change the whole socio-political debate. If they even win discourse hegemony they certainly impact on politics. Antonio Gramsci, and to some extent Jürgen Habermas are still right when they argue that the ruling ideas of the ruling class can be transformed by intellectual and popular discourses. It is a democratic duty of intellectuals to be a moral voice in society. In the case of the Serbian Institute for Philosophy and Social Theory, the support of the intellectuals was obviously a voice of morality and reason. Jürgen Habermas would call it the forceless force of the better argument.

Interview conducted by Gazela Pudar Draško

THE POLITICS OF FEAR:
THE RISE OF THE FAR RIGHT IN EUROPE
Ruth Wodak

Ruth Kodak is an Austrian linguist, Distinguished Professor Emeritus of Discourse at Lancaster University and linguistics at Vienna University, former president of European Linguistic Society, member of the European Academy and the British Academy of Social Sciences. Her research focuses on critical discourse analysis. In her work, she analyzes the various controversies surrounding globalization and the growing right-wing populism moving to the political center and European migration politics. She is the author of: *The politics of fear - what right wing populist discourse means* (2015), *The discourse of politics in action - politics as usual* (2011), *Discourse and discrimination* (2001), *Disorders of discourse* (1996). In 1996, she was awarded the Wittgenstein-Preis, the highest Austrian award in science, for her projects "Discourses on Un/employment in EU organizations; Debates on NATO and Neutrality in Austria and Hungary; The Discursive Construction of European Identities; Attitudes towards EU-Enlargement; Racism at the Top. Parliamentary Debates on Immigration in Six EU countries; The Discursive Construction of the Past - Individual and Collective Memories of the German Wehrmacht and the Second World War."

If we try to contextualize or label your research, what would you prefer: Discourse Studies (DS), Critical Discourse Analysis (CDA) or Discourse-Historical Approach?

I prefer Critical Discourse Studies, because it can encompass all of that. When I did my research in socio-linguistics, discourse studies did not yet exist, but since the 1990s, I've been working in this paradigm.

How do you perceive the growing networks and hubs of researchers within the DS and the changes in the CDA from the 1990s, following the symposium in Amsterdam in January 1991,1 where a few people, now considered important scholars in CDA, articulated some of the most important ideas significant for the development of the field?

Since the 1991 meeting in Amsterdam, Critical Discourse Studies developed fast and spread out. Very different approaches have been integrated, different research questions have been posed and within different interdisciplinary work areas. For example, some people have started working with people from education, like Günther Kress who came from the London School of Education. So, there exists an entire field which now investigates different genres, especially visual ones and now of course the Web 2.0. There is also a new development related to new technologies. And in the most recent issue of *Methods for Critical Discourse Studies* we included two new chapters on multi-modality and the Internet. The critical approach implies that you don't take anything for granted, you pose questions and endorse problem-oriented research, not focused only, for example, on metaphors or other linguistic elements.

The second development which is important concerns cognitive discourse studies, and how to integrate empirical work on the one

---

1   "The CDA as a network of scholars emerged in the early 1990s, following a small symposium in Amsterdam, in January 1991. Through the support of the University of Amsterdam, Teun van Dijk, Norman Fairclough, Gunther Kress, Theo van Leeuwen and Ruth Wodak spent two days together, and had the wonderful opportunity to discuss theories and methods of Discourse Analysis, specifically CDA. The meeting made it possible to confront with each other the very distinct and different approaches, which have, of course, changed significantly since 1991 but remain relevant, in many respect." In: Wodak, R. and Meyer, M. (2016). *Methods of Critical Discourse Studies* (3rd Edition). London: Sage.

hand and very formal abstract approaches, like Paul Chilton's work on *deixis,* or Piotr Cap's and Chris Hart's proximization theory. And then, there exists an approach, also strongly related to my own research, on discourse and argumentation, so argumentation theorists also participate in critical discourse studies. But there are also some tensions, which always appear in interdisciplinary work. Then we find another branch in language policy, which actually developed within sociolinguistics, as Critical Language Policy Studies, by, for example, Pennycook, Roberts and Monica Heller. I don't think they would actually want to be called Critical Discourse Studies (CDS) but we fit together very well. Moreover, other scholars are working with political science and with identity politics like myself. We work together with historians and political scientists. New problems always pop up for which you need different experts.

What is the position or status of DS within the Social Sciences? Do we speak about theory or different methodologies, or about both?

Sometimes there are various misunderstandings. One, for example, implies that DS or CDS are just "methods" or "tools" which you can apply. You analyze something like right-wing populism using a method which you take and apply to the text. This is not right because DS is always theory and methodology, at the same time. In every approach, there is a specific theory about discourse and society, whether it is the Frankfurt School or a Foucauldian, Gramscian or whatever kind of overall theory. But many people in the social sciences come to me and say: "How can I *do* CDA?" And then I say: "What do you mean? What do you want to do? What is your research question? What kind of approach do you endorse? How do you theorize communication and society?" And they say "Well, I just want to analyze this." Well, you cannot "just analyze this!" You have to have theoretical assumptions of how to approach social events and phenomena.

Another confusing, fallacious assumption maintains that you just analyze a text and you know what to do. Well, we don't just analyze texts. Obviously, we need to know a lot about contexts. You have to know some linguistics as well. You can't just interpret a text hermeneutically. Every text analysis is also hermeneutical, of course, but we have to deliver a *retroductable* analysis, so that somebody else can understand the procedure. You need to know pragmatics and/or semantics and/or rhetoric and so forth. Many social scientists don't like that. They tell me "Well, you know, you actually look at pronouns, inferences and implicatures, presuppositions, and we don't need this jargon! Everybody just knows language!" And then I counter, "But you also have a lot of jargon!" And linguists also have some jargon. Discourse studies is not a toolbox! That's why we work in an *abductive* way, we always go from theory to text and then back again to theory.

So, there are misunderstandings and whenever I teach in an interdisciplinary environment – which I have done a lot with political scientists, sociologists, historians, legal scholars and psychologists – they are disappointed. It is more difficult than they thought! They hope to find something like "Discourse Analysis Light." You j*ust find topoi*! Well, you don't just find *topoi*. You have to know something about argumentation theory. You don't have to study linguistics for 6 years; however, we are a problem-oriented paradigm, it depends what you are interested in. Then you develop an adequate methodology. I published an edited very useful book: *Qualitative Discourse Analysis in the Social Sciences* with Michal Krzyzanowski, one of my former students (and now professor at Uppsala University). Because we thought "ok, we have to provide an entry point for colleagues;" we developed an approach along different *genres*. How to analyze interviews, newspapers and dialogues for example. There are case studies in each chapter; and we present options how to proceed. So, if sociologists want to know how to analyze a debate, they will find it there without having to study two additional years.

And in your latest book Politics of Fear *your approach is discourse-historical. Did you develop this approach because you find it most appropriate for the problems you are analyzing (right-wing populism) or it is just a broader framework?*

We actually developed that a long time ago, with the study of the 'Waldheim Affair' from 1986 which involved the former UN General Secretary Kurt Waldheim. This scandal polarized the country. Waldheim had been involved with the *Wehrmacht* in Thessaloniki and in the Balkans, and he was the translator of General Alexander Löhr who had been one of the most vicious Nazi generals in Greece. In Thessaloniki (Salonika) more than forty thousand Jews were deported to the death camps. Waldheim wrote an autobiography, and this episode of his life didn't appear in the book. Journalists discovered that he had "forgotten" this part of his life, and huge investigations started. Quickly, an enormous wave of antisemitism in Austria followed as they said "Well, you know, he only did his duty like all of us did in *Wehrmacht*, the guilty people were Hitler and the SS and not ordinary soldiers." And this opinion polarized the country because suddenly the trope of *doing one's duty* was challenged: what did "fulfilling one's duty" mean in the context of an army that committed war crimes, extermination and genocide.

I was asked to investigate this debate and study the rise of antisemitism in this campaign. And I immediately understood that we needed a historical approach. There was no way we could just design a linguistic project because we had to understand the background, the war on the Balkans, and many insinuations. So, we needed psychologists to understand prejudices and historians to understand the history of antisemitism. And it became a huge project, although we had very little money and most colleagues conducted this research because it was so relevant. This was the first large post-war polarization of the Austrian society. 1986 in Austria was like 1968 in Germany: "What did your parents do during the war?" - the big question. And this led to the discourse-historical approach. It was obvious that the approach had to be interdisciplinary; we had to link our study to social change in a much more differentiated way than Fairclough did back in 1992 in *Discourse and Social Change*. We traced the entire discourse day by day, interview by interview. Finally, a book was published in Germany with the title *We Are All Innocent Perpetrators*. This had a huge impact – in Austria, however, it was denied. It was the first study of this kind, deconstructing xenophobia and antisemitism, the modern "stranger within," dealing with guilt and war crimes. This study triggered a significant change in my research orientation. It involved me very closely because I am a child of Austrian-Jewish refugees.

Other studies about 1989 and the fall of the Iron Curtain followed. We also conducted a study about Romanian and Polish migrants who came to Austria 1989 and '90, investigating the discursive shift from welcoming dissidents to rejecting migrants who would "take our jobs away." Then a study about Austrian identity followed which was translated into English, and a few projects about European identities and right-wing populism studies, triggered by the rise of Jörg Haider in 1986. 1986 is a tipping point in post-war Austria: for the first time the Nazi past was discussed, and then the *coup* by Haider in the Freedom Party, the extreme right becomes visible. Because of the rise of the FPÖ, we started analyzing Haider's historical revisionism, the appeal to the Nazis, provocations, xenophobia, anti-immigration, antisemitism, anti-Muslim sentiment, and the so forth. In 1999 Haider won a third of the votes (27%). I edited a book with Anton Pelinka *The Haider Phenomenon in Austria;* Austria was, like France, the first country where far-right populism became strong; the so-called *Haiderization* of Europe. Not only Haider's rhetoric but his concepts and ideology influenced many other right-wing populist and nationalist parties.

It seems that today far-right populist politics and its specific discourses and rhetoric have become part of the mainstream in many countries. It seems to me that this confirms your hypothesis from the Politics of Fear *about the "Heiderization", but also testifies to the changed relevance of right-wing populism, not just in Europe but worldwide. Why are we witnessing this normalization of the politics of fear, and what kind of shift has taken place within the discourses, political tools and political agenda of right-wing populism over the past years?*

I think it's important to state at the outset that in many ways our world has changed enormously between 2014 when I finished the first edition of the book, and 2020 when I finished the second edition. 2014, I took the European Parliament elections in 2014 as a point of departure, and in the second edition the EP-elections of 2019. These two points give us some insight into how European citizens have voted and how and what might have changed. Brexit and Trump's election were major events in this period which many people had not predicted. I was at the European University Institute in 2016 when the Brexit referendum took place, and people were shocked, nobody had expected this outcome among all the famous political scientists. Similar with Trump, very few people predicted that he would win. However, we have to keep in mind that there were socio-political contingencies which might explain why these elections and referenda turned out the way they did.

If you remember, I wrote an epilogue to the first edition when the *Alternative für Deutschland* was just emerging, and the first PEGIDA demonstrations were taking place; I asked the question "Who knows what Angela Merkel would do?," how will she react to this new movement from the far right, hoping of course that the CDU would distance itself from the far right and not try to overtake it like the Austrian People's Party had done, or Tories in the UK. Then, the refugee movement in 2015-6 occurred, a salient event, and intellectuals like Ivan Krastev, for example, claimed that this was *the* event that triggered the rise of the far right in Europe. I believe, it wasn't just the refugee movement, it was the aftermath of the financial crisis, people were very angry, and I think also rightly so, in the sense that the banks were saved but not the people. Don't forget the experience of the Eurozone crisis and the Greek crisis also in 2015, these were an important trigger for a shift to the right. For example, SYRIZA lost in the struggle against the Commission and the Troika. Then, he refugee movement, and all these crises facilitated an arena where many parties could position themselves. They opened a niche for the far right and the left. Obviously, the left did not use that opportunity to present an alternative program which could be juxtaposed to austerity politics (most left-wing parties unfortunately had followed the "third way"), and the far right instrumentalized migration and asylum policies. Thus, in most countries there now exists a polarization between urban-rural, more-less educated, old-young, female-male, there are many divisions and cleavages which have become much more apparent.

Thus, there are salient differences between 2014 and 2020; at the European elections the mainstream parties lost, and the extreme parties, left and right, won more seats, as well as the green parties. The latter can be explained by the rise of the "Fridays for Future" movement. Not only nationally, but also on a European level, people became much more aware of the looming climate crisis. Hence, there is a change in the political spectrum; refugees became scapegoats, labeled as "illegal migrants" (this is a wrong term, it should be "irregular migrants"), borders were closed; suddenly the debate focused "Fortress Europe," "we have to protect our borders." The "Balkan Route" was the centerpiece in the (Austrian) debate. Thus, this agenda was colonized by the far right and normalized by the conservative mainstream. Not everywhere, but in some countries – Austria is a good example, basically the ÖVP was taken over by Sebastian Kurz, it's now the "new" People's Party, with a very restrictive asylum and migration agenda. They colonized the topics of the far right, and 10% of their voters. In other words, they adopted the politics of the Austrian Freedom Party in respect to migration, asylum and human rights.

This is similar to experiences in the UK where the Tories took over UKIP's topics. UKIP basically doesn't exist anymore, although there are other far right and extremist parties. Of course, it's very difficult to explain why Donald Trump won, there are many books and papers about that, so I will not try to give *the* explanation. On the one hand, it was a racist backlash against eight years of a "black man in the White House" (Barack Obama), many middle class male and female white voters rejected that. Migration issues were instrumentalized, the threat of being invaded was mobilized by Trump. In spite of Trump's misogyny and obvious sexism, many women voted for Trump. Studies illustrate that paradox happened because immigration and asylum policies were perceived more important than sexism.

Third, there are economic reasons; however, a new book by Aaron Winter and Aurelien Moundon shows that the working class did not entirely vote for Trump, because the working class has changed. In the US, the majority of the working class are poor people from ethnic minorities. The result of the elections show that these parts of the working class voted for Clinton, or didn't vote at all. The same is true of the European elections. The "classic" working class does not exist anymore in many countries, the working class now are migrants. In Vienna for example, at the elections in October 2020, one third of the population of Vienna did not have the right to vote because they are not Austrian citizens, they are migrants. These people are not represented anymore, not even by the trade unions, and the same is true about the precariat, there is nobody to represent them and they are frequently endangered.

Thus, simple explanations don't work. Moreover, Trump also succeeded because he is charismatic and an entertainer. He persuaded and mobilized big turnouts of people and addressed them with his anti-foreigner and anti-elite rhetoric. And Clinton's utterance about the "deplorables", her e-mail scandal, the intervention by Russia, tall these are important factors as well. The traditional left, I believe, has not really understood these changes. I might just add that it is obvious that certain topics and ways of expression are normalized if they are used by mainstream parties. If topics are colonized by the mainstream conservatives, then far right rhetoric is also integrated. It is frequently more coded. There is important work by Wilhelm Heitmeyer, a German sociologist who proposes the concept of "coarse civility:" how the middle-class talk now; without the support of the conservatives, the far right would never have succeeded.

One widespread "one-size-fits-all" explanation for the success of right-wing populism suggests that it presents the "wrong answer to real problems" in conditions of a lack of real political alternative, i.e., that it is fueled by the grievances of the "left-behind" social strata produced by neoliberalization. However, you have pointed out that examples such as Austria and Switzerland, wealthy nations in which the devastating consequences of neoliberalization are not widely felt but in which right-wing populism thrives nevertheless, challenge this thesis. Would you argue that there is some kind of "lowest common denominator" in right-wing populism across the globe that, despite all the contextual differences, could account for (some of) its success – is it something in the way right-wing populism uses language to render reality "manageable" in conditions of modernity (along the lines of Foucault's notion of knowledge/power)?

Why do Austria, Switzerland and Denmark for example, very rich countries, have huge parties on the far right – Norway as well, the richest country on Earth? All these countries were not heavily struck by the financial crisis. This phenomenon relates to identity politics and symbolic politics. It's not coincidental that these are small countries within the bigger European Union (except for Switzerland and Norway), in these countries national identity politics go back a long way. The nostalgia for a heroic past, a "retrotopia," as Zygmunt Baumann calls it, is apparent. This is certainly the case in Austria, Switzerland and Denmark. Then the dystopia with which these far-right parties mobilize, the threat that the "real" Austrians, Hungarians, Finns or Danes will die out, that their language and culture will die out, that they are being "replaced" - that's where the identitarians come in, this is part of their rhetoric and has always been, it goes back to the Nazi concept of *Umvolkung*.

Thus, the danger is invoked that we, the "real" people are threatened by outsiders, or by the "strangers from within." There's a danger from the inside and the outside, a danger from the top – the elite – and from below, the "lazy" people. If you create such a dystopian scenario, you can legitimatize the claim that you have to defend yourself, that you have to fight. There is a "logic" implying that you have to protect the Christian Occident, the "real" people, against the strangers from within, the Muslims, the Jews, other ethnic minorities, strangers from outside, refugees, illegal migrants, from elites on top and the beggars or homeless people below. Creating such a scenario is part of the "politics of fear."

The second explanation is "the fear of losing out." In Austria, Switzerland, Norway and Denmark, in all these rich countries, the middle class and lower middle class are not convinced anymore that their children will have a better life than they do. It's obvious that people are afraid of losing out, they haven't lost out yet but they are frightened. And if you are confronted by such dystopian scenarios, then it is easy to develop a nostalgia for something that was much better – even though these homogeneous nation states never existed. Then you mobilize people by saying "we have to protect what we have," which is why the asylum and migration laws are so restrictive; in Austria there is also the emphasis on the German language. And the Danes, as we know from opinion polls, are supposed to be the happiest people on Earth, so they want to protect that. Hungary and Poland are different because there the far-right parties are the majority in government.

The move to the far right can also be explained by the common denominator of "law and order" politics, where you need a savior for the men and women on the street. And it doesn't matter if Trump is actually a billionaire, he can be perceived as a role model ("he made it"). Another common denominator is nativism. During the Covid crisis governments returned to a virulent nationalism and nativism – who "belongs" to Hungary, Austria, Poland etc. Nativism, ethno-nationalism is the most important denominator: "make Austria, America, Serbia great again." Anti-elitism is another aspect which is common to all those parties – the elites can vary, they can be liberals, the managers, the opposition party, the universities, Washington (for Donald Trump), the Wall Street, journalists, fake news producers, the EU. Coupled with this (but this is not the case everywhere) are conservative values. You have very conservative family values in Poland, linked to Catholicism. There are huge struggles over abortion, gender, family values. Orban even proposed a new law that Hungarian women should give birth to more "Hungarian" children. This related to the traditional "blood and soil ideology." But, of course, such values would not be acceptable in Scandinavian countries or the Netherlands. There are different agendas in different countries.

There is much talk on the left today of the need to construct a "counter-hegemonic bloc" as a precondition for winning political power and as a bulwark against the sliding of the political space to the right. This would require the left to reshape the network of discourses that constitute the "dominant ideology" of a naturalized market liberalism and (ethnic or territorial) nationalism in most contemporary nation states – in your terms it would mean the "setting of alternative frames and agendas". However, in fighting this "symbolic war," the left has shown limited capacity for a strategic use of language, as it seems to rely too much on what you define as the legitimizing techniques of moral evaluation *and* rationalization, *and not enough on* mythopoesis *(legitimation through the telling of stories), which seems to be particularly important when one tries to set alternative frames and agendas. Would you have any advice for the left in terms of its politics of discourse?*

I added some points to the second edition of *Politics of Fear* – the media are important, the way provocation and scandalization are instrumentalized by the far right, and the media play along. And if you leave so much attention to this recurring pattern, you do not have the space to set your own agenda. Thus, creating space and establishing a coalition with some media, a kind of *cordon sanitaire*, would be salient: not every tweet and every provocation by Trump should make headlines on the first page. Why does the AFD have to be invited to every talk show when they only hold 11 percent of votes? There is an excellent study Helene Coffé, where she compares the regional elections in Flanders and Wallonia, which both have a social-democratic party. In Flanders the party lost, because it integrated the far-right policies into its agenda. In Wallonia the social democrats succeeded in establishing a *cordon sanitaire* with the media: the media did not report on the far right or only little. This worked and the social democrats won, with their agenda of equality, human rights and so forth, with the help of the media.

Moreover, you cannot win if you don't have an agenda. You have to have a program which you can juxtapose to the agenda of the conservatives and the far right. You have to provide a social equality agenda, and consider the new working class, the new proletariat and precariat, and integrate the trade unions. In Austria these are like dinosaurs, there is nothing for the precariat, for example; and you have to use a persuasive rhetoric. There is much to learn from the fact that you have to be *genre oriented*. If you have posters, you can't place huge arguments on them because nobody reads a poster for five minutes, you have to have good provocative images or slogans. You will also have to simplify some complex arguments in the posters, because that's inherent in the genre. If you have a brochure with the program, there you can spell it out. The left really should learn some linguistics, that genres and texts inherently require different linguistic realizations; you cannot distribute programs which are 50 pages long, nobody will read that. You have to have 5 points and develop them.

What I also write about that in the last chapter of my book; you should call things by their proper names. If somebody is racist, you have to say he's racist and provide evidence. You shouldn't use inflationary terms like "fascist" - everybody's now a fascist – you will just be taken to court. If you say something like that, you have to have evidence (like in the case of AfD's Björn Höcke). But on the other hand, you shouldn't be vague. There also currently exist debates which are distracting people on the left from the main focus, which is the fight for a better life for all citizens in a country, not only for the "pure" Serbs or Austrians, and that's what the left should do.

Finally, last year you joined the international support for the Institute for Philosophy and Social Theory in Belgrade, which fought (ultimately successfully) for the preservation of its academic autonomy. Do you believe that intellectuals can make a difference, and if so, what kind?

First of all, science and all kinds of intellectual enterprises like your Institute have to be autonomous. That's part of the fundamental rights agenda – press freedom, freedom of opinion and of science – that's a basic right. All our countries have signed these fundamental rights. If somebody challenges this, wants to take it away, of course you have to struggle against it. Second, intellectuals do work, discuss and provide explanations and predictions about very complex social problems and issues. This work is important because if we don't understand and cannot contextualize phenomena, big mistakes could happen and do happen. Third, I believe in the Enlightenment and that we do learn from the past or from failures. And, as people who work with knowledge, we have to continue to educate our students, etc.

If you teach in universities or write books, and so forth, this is very important because self-reflection allows societies to develop in different ways – and *post hoc*, we can explain why things happened and why one should or should not take specific decisions. Intellectuals should protect their autonomous position because otherwise they are in danger of being used. Hannah Arendt already wrote in her essays about lies and truth in politics that some intellectuals may allow themselves to be instrumentalized and this is dangerous. But intellectuals who position themselves as autonomous are extraordinarily important – if you don't have self-reflection on this basis things *just happen*, and grave mistakes might be repeated.

Interview conducted by Dušan Ristić and Marjan Ivković

IN SEARCH OF NEW WORDS

WHAT IS ORDINARY FEMINISM?
Fabienne Brugère

Fabienne Brugère is a French philosopher specializing in aesthetics and philosophy of art, history of modern philosophy, moral and political philosophy, Anglo-American philosophy and feminist theory. She was a professor at Bordeaux-Montaigne University and vice-president for international relations at this university. She joined Paris VIII University in 2014, as chair of "philosophy of modern and contemporary art." In the same year, she was a candidate on the Socialist Party's list. Since 2019 she has been president of the University Paris Lumières. In 2015 she was awarded the Legion of Honour. She is the author of: *Theory of Art and Philosophy of Sociability according to Shaftesbury* (1999), *It's too Beautiful* (2008), *Questions of Respect: Survey on Contemporary Figures of Respect, The Ethics of Care* (2011), *The New Spirit of Liberalism* (2011), *The Politics of the Individual* (2013), and *The End of Hospitality* (with Guillaume Le Blanc, 2017).

Autonomy, an ethical value par excellence, has today been put to bad ends. It would appear that in shrinking, all the qualities of the political subject are dissipating behind forms of life stripped to the point of mere survival. All illusion of mastery has disappeared. Nevertheless, if the epidemic has revealed vulnerabilities, its handling has erased democracy and social care to the advantage of national sovereignty, radicalization of borders, which we have strengthened everywhere, and the reinforcement of the disciplinary paradigm. And beyond the nationalization of the virus, there is still the possibility to think the transnational global community, based on the experienced of a shared vulnerability. How should this thought emerge, this ethics of care in the national context, for it to be taken seriously and truly meant globally? Is it not finally time to think a politics of care? That is, a true enlargement of the political community?

Much has happened that supports the idea that the global health crisis has made it necessary to rethink our national autonomy in relation to our vital needs. A new consensus being developed at the moment intends to articulate economic patriotism and a society of care. Faced with an unexpected halt to the world economy, as was the case in 2020, what we could see is that countries that still produced industrial goods were the best at handling the pandemic (Chinese masks and medications, German respirators, American and English vaccines, etc.). However, economic patriotism can quickly devolve into "each for themselves." It brought back the topic of national sovereignty and magically revitalized the sovereign subject. In calling for a return to strong borders, it reinscribed the social state into a national one: it created the conditions for a new nationalism, lapsing into a discourse of grandiose illusions, such as "Make America Great Again" of the former President Trump.

The COVID-19 pandemic has not placed us all equally before the illness. The latest symptom of this inequality is the difference in access to vaccines from country to country. Further, even within a given nation, there are inequalities based on where we live, our gender, our socio-economic status. In such conditions, how could the renewal of the social state take exclusively the political form of the nation state? How could paying attention to others, taking care of them be made compatible with a closed society, or one filled with national egoism? In effect, we are assisting the piling up of vulnerabilities that make us globally more exposed: how do we continue to live without all the medication, equipment, and simple accessories (such as clothes and shoes) produced in China? What can we do for the countries that have not been able to produce the vaccine without the help of the scientifically and industrially more advanced? Our lives have been non-sovereign. The closure into national lives is an illusion of sovereignty.

The pandemic has revealed a kernel of enormous precariousness. A general uncertainty, incapacity to think into the future. We are protecting certain categories of people, while plunging others into fatal situations. Hope has been jeopardized, in particular for your people. A whole generation seems paralyzed by precariousness and catastrophe. More than ever, there is a feeling of being exposed to the unknown. How can we adequately address this problem?

I am not sure that we are having an unprecedented experience: the plagues of the seventeenth century, the Spanish flu in Europe at the end of the First World War, the Hong Kong flu in the summer of 1968, or even the SARS-CoV-1 epidemic in Asia at the beginning of this century all had divisions of populations similar to those now, a renewed interest in public health, sanitary measures (such as mask-wearing). What is without precedent is the complete halt of the world economy everywhere at the same time, covered by the global media, as well as the omnipresence of the possibility of digital communication, their power multiplied many times over by the GAFA companies (Google, Apple, Facebook, Amazon). It has resulted in the digital sphere and its paradigm to be more visible than ever before. As Bernard Harcourt wrote in *Exposed*, our lives are exposed on social networks, formatted by algorithms, whether we like it or not. What will constitute our liberties from now on? They need to be rethought.

And I am not certain that the youth is so completely deprived of a future. First of all, there is not one youth, but youths. Between the youth of wealthy and middle classes in rich countries and the young migrants who leave Sub-Saharan Africa, or war-torn countries plunged into chaos, such as Afghanistan or Syria, forms of life are very different. In Western Europe at least there is a portion of the youth, generally well-educated, who believe in feminist struggles and fighting a political ecological fight. Of course, the world is still split, unjust, subject often to extreme exploitation of resources or primary materials. It needs fixing, and we are living these infinite tasks to the youth. In terms of heritage, we could have collectively done much better.

How do you see the difference between charity and care? Is charity merely a capitalist, neoliberal invention, allowing us to keep our distance from the Other, to delegate away the work of care? We know now that it is imperative to take care of the ill, the old, the young, the poor, but also the climate, biodiversity, and institutions. And yet, all these activities are in crisis to the extent that they are underfunded, ties that hold those most fragile are frayed, individualized, unrecognized, and privatized. Each individual is responsible only for their own relations of care. This crisis of care, is it due to institutional structures of capitalist societies? Separate to politics and the economy?

Charity is in no way originally neoliberal; it was successfully combined with neoliberalism for the sake of coexistence of the financial capitalist world and a conservative use of religion. It is an old idea or Christian practice that takes its meaning from the following formula: "Love thy neighbor as thyself," or as the Evangelist John says "Love one another." Charity certainly contains something beautiful and almost superhuman: love of all others. This love is the completion of divine law, necessarily given to us from something above and beyond human: God. The ethics and politics of care are much more modest. They describe a state of society in terms of taking care of others (children, the ill, the old, etc.) or the planet, and ask whether these relations, when constrained by institutions, the market, a system of governance, are sufficient? Often, they are found wanting and cannot address a crisis of care. Thus, theories of care become normative in search of transforming relations, for a better future. The latest book by Eva Feder Kittay, *Learning from My Daughter: The Value and Care of Disable Minds* is indicative in this way, as it affirms the importance of a "normativity of care" to be integrated into all processes by which we "take care" of others in the world.

Of course, where neoliberal ideology comes in, and needs to be opposed, is the reduction of all responsibility to the individual. We know how the Reagan presidency in the US and the Thatcher government in the UK have given life to the idea that the poor are personally responsible for their situation, while society gave the resources to all to become successful individuals. We are all tied to one another, and life's accidents and challenges do not strike us all equally based on our social class, country of residence, ethnic origin, or indeed our gender.

You recently published a book entitled On ne naît femme, on le devient *(2019), in which you write "Only ordinary feminism exists, done through the voices and stories of women," and also "Western imperialist feminism does not exist. It is not feminism." You insist on a feminism for all women, an ordinary feminism that considers the reality of women dependent on their geographic, cultural, and economic context (70% of the global poor are women). In addition, you present the novel idea that the hormonal body demands to be considered within the history of woman, take its place in society, once it is no longer a reproductive body. Do these two approaches allow to reignite contemporary feminism?*

An ordinary feminism will be the great project of the twenty-first century: women want real emancipation that would change their daily lives, whether they live in Paris, New York, Buenos Aires or Lagos. They will tolerate less and less forms of oppression exerted on their lives every day, and will say more and more: in the name of what is half of humanity plunged into servitude? Emancipation of women has already been announced with the #MeToo movement, women's marches in Argentina and Poland, the rebellion of women in Iran, in Kurdistan, or indeed the presence of feminists in the most recent protests in Algeria. All the world knows that this revolution is coming. For this reason, the various forms of patriarchal oppression are organizing, globalizing, gathering more than ever, to defend the old order.

In the face of such a global offensive, feminists of all countries need to unite. The philosopher Judith Butler defines feminism as a "coalition of differences." This project needs to be taken up once again. A word that has been broadly denounced, yet is interesting, is "sisterhood," in the sense of solidarity among women. The historian Arlette Farge has shown clearly how women's solidarity developed in the seventies, and how it has stubbornly remained broken down along class and individual lines since then. The big question with which women are confronted today is the social question, this unavoidable reality of difference in power and wealth in the world. The differences are not only in skin color, but among strata of social living, freedom of movement or in speaking one's mind, struggling: between the top echelons (whether in Europe or in Africa) and exiled undocumented women or those living on the street, there is often no solidarity. Between a Danish woman whose studies are financed by the government and the Bulgarian or Romanian woman in the lowest rung of salary in Europe, there is no solidarity. These solidarities must be created in the feminism of the future.

A life of struggle is today weakened by a brutal individualism and an exploitation of the world's resources more aggressive than ever before. Feminist discourse must not become rigid or splinter. Today's feminisms must once again take up the universal, that is, develop a solidarity of women with respect to women, of men with respect to women, and the wealthy with respect to the poor. This is the project before us of an ordinary feminism that affirms liberty and equality of women, that struggles against all religious, political, militaristic, and sexual attempts to subjugate women. "Sisterhood" is the search for justice for women who are ignored, for whom there is no justice.

Simone de Beauvoir wrote that "the future remains largely open," on condition we prepare it with regard to forms of life that affect us. Another condition is to take into consideration the different ages of life. This is what I wished to do in *On ne naît pas femme, on le devient*. Beauvoir insisted on the different forms of oppression of women depending on their age and context. Menopause remains a largely ignored topic among feminists, still taboo because it reintroduces the hormonal body, that is, important changes in the universal matter of women. We must think it while always keeping in mind the particularity of feminism, its plurality, that the body is not exhausted by its social or cultural representations: it is a lived body, hormonal, with its own sense of its visualization, which we can always model, transform, submit to surgical operations, etc.

Was the possibility of sexually aggressive behavior ignored in the name sexual liberation that took place after 1968? Is there a violent element in the expression of desire, or brutality in its liberation? Gabriel Matzneff's appeal published on November 26, 1977 in Le Monde and the following day in Libération, "L'enfant, l'amour, l'adulte," has resurfaced. Staggeringly pro-pedophilic, signed by some sixty intellectuals, including Bernard Kouchner, Jack Lang, Jean-Paul Sartre, Simone de Beauvoir, Roland Barthes, Gilles and Fanny Deleuze, André Glucksmann. Fifteen days later, the newspaper published several responses to this "unscrupulous defense of vice." Does this not mean that it was not merely a matter of spirit of the times?

I have not written much on the context of the Matzneff appeal. I would, first of all, say that these intellectuals and philosophers were not infallible, that they are not always right about everything; they too can be subject to the fashion of the times and opinion, they can overestimate their knowledge on a given subject. For example, Rousseau wrote wonderful texts when it came to criticizing property relations or on the possibility of direct democracy. But it is distressing when he writes on women in Book V of *Emile*, where Sophie is described as the person who ought to be deferential towards Emile, which is to say, not too knowledgeable, remaining primarily in the service of her husband.

It is uncontestable that our societies have become more ethical, more haunted by the idea of decency. We can see this in what is in France called "the Polanski affair." The filmmaker remains protected by the cinema world in France, which accepted him with open arms when he was expelled from the United States for the rape of a minor in 1977, a case which the American justice system refuses to close. When he was once again accused of rape once again at the opening of his film "J'accuse" on November 13, 2019, the moral condemnation in France became widespread, and the public largely heard what the feminists had to say. What is surprising, from an ethical stance, is the protection Roman Polanski enjoys in the French cinema world, in which he has cult status. There is a veil of silence and an impossibility to listen, because in this milieu his stature is that of a "great man," which would be tarnished by the words of the victims. It is protection of a system, which must be called patriarchal, structured by a strong masculinity and weak femininity. It is very problematic in terms of justice: all the viewpoints should be heard, regardless of their greatness in the world of cinema. Victims should have the right to protection in a democracy, or at the very least it is necessary to listen to women who claim to be victims before any judgment.

The #MeToo movement has globally given women more freedom to speak out. It has revealed how central sexuality is in the system of oppression of women and the necessity to put an end to rape culture. How can we make sure not to succumb to expeditive justice that would alienate men from the women's cause?

We are everywhere in the world far from any expeditive justice that would alienate men from the women's cause. The problem does not lie there; rather, how to make people hear the oppressed voices of women? How can we bring down the rising numbers of femicide case (currently in France), with a government that is incapable of taking measures against such crimes?

The #MeToo movement has amplified women's voices in the whole world from its inception (which was in 2007 by Tarana Burke denouncing sexual violence done to Black women in the United States). These women (but also other groups constituted of minorities, such as gay people, child incest victims, etc.) did not merely denounce their aggressors, they came together as an assembly of voices, which was none other than the construction of a space of subjectivation. We know this, the women's voices could be heard because they turned their vulnerability at being exposed to men's violence into the power of acting together, a collective strength.

There has been a constitution of women's voices taking place through this reversal, a reversal of shame, but this process surpasses shame. The feeling of shame is at the heart of the texts written by women sexually assaulted within the Weinstein affair in Hollywood.

More broadly, we need to remember that victims of harassment or rape feel shame for it, for being turned into an object for male sexual enjoyment. Shame often makes the denunciation of the committed acts impossible. And when such words finally do come, they often go unheard or are considered without merit. Nevertheless, it is interesting to see how this shame has been turned around: the victims have become the accusers by using the Internet. Shame has switched camps: by publicly recounting what took place, the shame of having been attacked is transformed into the shame of revelation of the attacker's dirty secrets. Has this shame reignited a resistance, or specifically a feminist resistance? Will it bring about new relations between men and women? Does it formulate the voices of women, ordinary voices of women (because harassment concerns all women)? Certainly; yet, there is something else tied to what the virtual community has created that goes well beyond this initial shame. It is the unique taking up of each woman's voice to create a collective voice (amplified by each individual voice with it), without this collective voice denying the singularity of each constitutive voice. Rather, it becomes the structure through which each voice can be deployed as a unique voice.

By constituting this virtual assembly of women, an equality of masculine and feminine voices becomes possible, become conceivable. Analyzing "women's voices" is a task of political philosophy. It goes without saying that such analysis cannot but be conducted by leaving behind all essentialization or normative ideals that postulate unity within the category of "woman." What then can women's voices bring about? 1) They can design a practice of subjectivation rather than designate subjects who merely carry a naturalized identity. 2) They can bring an anti-foundationalist approach that leaves behind all questions of origin. Thus, everything is conditional (the unconditional does not exist), which leads to defend coalition politics that privileges horizontal relations over vertical ones, by way of using the power of gender and listening to all excluded voices.

We live on this warming planet with more than seven billion other people. The cosmopolitan enthusiasm is no longer a luxury, but a necessity. Do we have to believe that we will be saved in order to act? Or do we act more ethically and efficiently if we do not know the end of history? This would mean the emergence of a new kind of political solidarity, not limited to the nation. A philosophy as counter-culture. Acts of solidarity now occur between different peoples, on various levels of vulnerability, even between different species, all in a world of increased destruction and recourse to the identitary. This requires much more than a will, a vision, a philosophy. What can philosophy do in the face of such challenges?

We are, all of us, men and women, fundamentally vulnerable. It is an anthropological fact that cannot be hidden. The COVID-19 pandemic has made this vulnerability particularly visible. Definitions of the human that draw on vulnerability call into question the tenacity of the all-powerful and independent individual, as well as theories of the social contract and sovereignty as they were used in the seventeenth and eighteenth centuries starting with Hobbes and Locke. The sovereign individual is a fiction. Yet, the refusal to think of individuals as fundamentally vulnerable is profoundly anchored in our various collective narratives. On the one hand, the birth of political liberalism and its revival all the way to John Rawls, pose an ideal of autonomy and sovereignty all forms of dependence and vulnerability is considered as a loss of mastery or rationality, an impossibility to decide correctly, which is to say, participate in public matters. Richard Sennett talks about how political liberalism has glorified the perspective of a free subject, forgetting that autonomy is not decree and that it does not concern every single moment of a life: "The dignity of dependence has never appeared in liberalism as a valuable political project." On the other hand, the development of neoliberal ideas, analyzed by Michel Foucault and many others since, elaborate a norm of an individual performer capable of subjecting all spheres of life to those of the market. Personal calculation, which rationalizes interest, becomes omnipresent to the point of glorifying individual responsibility as the sole source of responsibility. Such reasoning says that being poor can be alleviated by individual conduct: the poor person is alone responsible for their situation. Thus, social services are obsolete and are turned into services for paying customers. What, then, can we do with this essentially interdependent individual, characteristic of globalization and its domino effects? The ethics of care is focused on the present: an interdependent, interconnected world, in which relations are not limited to narrow selfish interests, which is not there for humans to merely develop from birth: we cannot live without care, without attention, without support of others and collective structures, nor without taking into consideration the environment. Institution are good for the individuals when they support and promote solidarity of some towards others, inclusion, rather than exclusion. Equally, we dream more and more of nature, with endless urban sprawl terrifying us. The relations between oneself and others, between oneself and the Earth are being re-examined. Care is therefore an interesting model, as it valorizes horizontal relations rather than centralizing verticality. Good care consists of inhabiting a world with one's own subjectivity, imagination, affects, but also being suspicious of all markers of power. It means learning and recognizing differences, building worlds for the sake of an always modifiable common, with newcomers, and with our environment. The work of Philippe Descola has taught us the extent to which the West has enclosed itself around the idea that humans live in a world separate from that of non-humans. Today, care participates in resisting this kind of human supremacy, joining ecological struggles from the point of view of, on the one hand, the foregrounding of interdependencies and vulnerabilities that place us all in relation to the Earth, and on the other, a deconstruction of all the sundry forms of human mastery over the world: the productive over those giving care, men over women, humans over non-humans. The resistance has been formulated in the expression of a "different voice," as Carol Gilligan defines it in her studies on the contours of an ethics of care: "the different voice is a voice of resistance" to dualities and hierarchies. Let us be different to one another and find commonalities, unifying points, coalitions, for the sake of a society as democratic as we can make it.

You have been active in numerous social movements for democracy and freedom. Recent among these struggles was that of the Institute for Philosophy and Social Theory in Serbia, for which you joined the international support, which yielded positive results. Do you think that intellectuals can make a difference in society and if so, what kind? What, in your opinion, is the role and place of intellectuals in contemporary societies and social struggles?

Intellectuals are above all holders of knowledge acquired from books, works of art, field studies, archives, or indeed lab experiments. They attempt to advance via a relation to knowledge, which makes them at once triumphant and humble. In a way they seek what is just or true. They make a difference through their knowledge, but free of arrogance, without assuming a haughty position. They are able to intervene in current debates and social struggles based on their domain of expertise.

However, they are also citizens, ordinary inhabitants of a given country. In this sense, without their particular expertise, they can, like anyone, be part of some collective, some social movement, or political party. Like anyone could, in the name of democracy, justice, freedom, equality.

Kant's saying in *What is Enlightenment?* remains current and valid: *sapere aude*, dare to know, dare to use your own head. The intellectual, more than anyone else, should not remain closed within their prejudices or mere opinion. Sometimes, they might get entangled, but their life must be spent using vigilance and setting high standards.

Interview conducted by Zona Zarić

REDUCING LIFE TO BIOLOGICAL LIFE
Guillaume Le Blanc

Guillaume Le Blanc is a French philosopher and writer who has written some twenty books, many of which have been translated into several languages. He previously taught at Paris-Est Créteil (where he held the Chair of Practical Philosophy) and Bordeaux-Montaigne universities and is currently Professor of political and social philosophy at the Paris Diderot University. His work focuses on the question of "social critique" and the creativity of ordinary lives as a reinvention of norms. More specifically, he studies the complex limits that distinguish precariousness, exclusion, decent life and normality. The legacy of Foucault and Canguilhem is here accomplished in the direction of a reformulation of social philosophy. His publications include *Les maladies de l'homme normal* (2004); *Vies ordinaires, vies précaires* (2007); *L'invisibilité sociale* (2009), *Que faire de notre vulnérabilité* (2011), among which novels *Sans domicile fixe* (2004), *Courir : Méditations physiques* (2012), *Vaincre nos peurs, tendre la main, Mobilisons-nous pour les exclus!* (2019).

Since when has public health been a legitimate reason to curb freedoms? Has humanity ever known epidemics without also drastically curtailing freedoms?

I am not sure that public health was ever a legitimate reason to curb freedoms. I would rather say that public health was a construction whose legitimation implies suspension of liberties. Which is not exactly the same, and it is what we have seen today in the current crisis. A fundamental distinction to be made is between health and public health. We need to examine the process of valorization of health: it only becomes of value when it is tested by illness. As long as I am not sick, I do not know I am in good health. It is simply fact until it becomes a matter of urgency. Leriche wrote that "health is living with silently functioning organs." When the noise of a sick body interrupts this state of affairs, health becomes a value to be reclaimed. Yet, this reclaiming can never go back to how it was. Regaining one's health means having gone through the experience of illness. Once we feel in good health again, we know that health is a precarious value. Individual valorization of health comes with the knowledge of its precariousness. This is an existential process. It can be summed up by two essential traits, which Canguilhem has formulated particularly well in *La santé, concept vulgaire question scientifique*. The first: health is a feeling well before it is known; we feel in good health without really knowing whether we are. And the second: health is a motivating value tied to the possibility of removing oneself from life norms and inventing new ones.

Obviously, there is a difference between personal health and public health. It is less of an individual feeling and more a construction in relation to a population. It is less a value than a calculation of a whole set of physical, psychological, social, and economic facts. To speak of public health is to admit that the individual notion of health also impacts the population as a whole, and by extension, political powers that be charged to guarantee it. In 1946, the World Health Organization (WHO) defined it as "a state of complete physical, mental, and social well-being, not limited to the absence of illness or infirmity." There is, thus, this idea of power of the public to control the state of life of a population, to control the illness within it. Of course, this has always been a question of political sovereignty. Starting in the sixteenth and seventeenth centuries, very strict measures were taken to fight the plague epidemics in Europe. In *A Journal of a Plague Year* from 1722, the English novelist Daniel Defoe recounts the quarantining of sick people, under very strict conditions. The surveillance laws of a plagued city were described meticulously by Foucault in *Discipline and Punish*, giving rise to a most prohibitive version of discipline, which he calls "discipline-blockade:" strict regulation, quartering of urban space, each street surveilled by agents, rationalization of pathways and means of provision distribution – an art of social quarantine is established in the midst of a plague epidemic. This archaic disciplinary technology, relying on surveillance agents and daily reporting on the numbers of dead has lasted until today. The paradox described by Foucault is that a disciplinary government for epidemics culminates in "social quarantine," leading to biopolitics and public health. The extreme disciplining of social space has had the consequence of suspension of a whole slew of liberties – this is the domain of biopolitics. For Foucault, we have transitioned from a sovereignty defined by the law of the sword, the ability "to take life or let live," into an age of biopolitics, where the essential is "to foster life or disallow it to the point of death." This change poses questions of possibility of death in a biopolitical age – which is what Foucault gleans from references to racism (depreciating the biological life of a population is the condition of having the power to destroy it) – revealing an administration of life without precedent, in which it would be admissible, in the name of life, to raze all the values of liberty, without which life is not possible. The biopolitical paradox is as follows: the biological enters the redefinition of the political, since the latter sought to deal with mortality and fertility rates, life expectancy, taking measures against accidents at work, social protection – all in the name of public health. All of which is a good thing, but becomes the ultimate sacred that the political must honor by all means. Preserving life becomes the new political imperative, at the cost of the erasure of values which alone give meaning to life, that is, at the cost of reducing life to biological life. I cannot help but think that this reduction is exactly the price of life in the West, and I cannot help but think that the price was paid by indifference to life beyond the West.

Certain public personalities are worried that "protection of life" is conducted at all cost, that is, to the detriment of our liberties. What is your opinion on this debate? Supposed sanctity of life hides its debasement, its degradation. As you describe in your book La fin de l'hospitalité, *written with Fabienne Brugère (2017), hospitality follows from a presupposition of the vulnerability of all people. Should it not then be defended in the same way whenever it is endangered, famously in the example of the precarious lives of migrants?*

The good thing that this crisis has made evident is the raw fact of the inequality of protection. The sanctity of life is really the sanctity of the Western form of life, endangered by those towards whom we could have been indifferent, as it seemed to us in the case of other viruses, such as Ebola, that they were the viruses of "others." To the extent that our mental cartography implies a radical frontier, psychologically lived as fact, between "our" First World and "their" Fourth World, epidemics seemed to us, prior to this crisis, far away, related to forms of life too close to certain natural environments, or bound to medical science of a previous age. When the epidemic struck our world, we were loath to revise our whole mental map in the face of our discovery that we are equally vulnerable to a virus that knew no borders. There was a brief moment of radical global equality, interestingly, but it did not last; rather, we reconstituted ourselves very quickly to accept a discourse of protection. The First World, although equally vulnerable, recreated borders with which we thought we could purchase protection as we were inside these borders, but which also represented an epic struggle for all the people who it excluded. The vertiginously high mortality at this moment in India shows us the extreme inequality of the global vaccine response to the virus. Thus, life has become a universality to be unconditionally protected across the globe at the same moment when protection has presented itself as the very instrument of powers recreating borders and conditions of inequal life in all the ways implied by those borders. These barriers between the First and the Fourth World are absolute. Yet, they also reveal other fault lines of inequality of protections against forces that endanger life. Thus, effectively, the protection we should extend to endangered lives, either vitally or politically imperiled, are largely dependent on our capacity to understand another's life as a life and even potentially as mine. From this standpoint, the current migration crisis only heightens the differences between lives worthy of being protected and those not. In the face of these inequalities, hospitality is simply a turn to philanthropic emergency of care and towards an appeal of compassion as private will; it is not, however, understood as a political structure of accommodation, on the basis of which we might ask anew the question of political affiliation. I revisit these three modes of hospitality – caring, accommodating, and belonging – in my book *Vaincre nos peurs et tendre la main. Mobilisons-nous pour les exclus* (2019).

Since the publication of your book Vies ordinaires, vies précaires *(2007), you have defined and worked on the concept of precariousness. Along with Judith Butler in the United States, you are one of the first to work on this question. What is the difference between poverty and precariousness? Is it a social or psychological state? Does it affect subjective capacities of those who suffer it? An intermediary state between inclusion and the path of exclusion? Why is precariousness doubly interesting? And what of the gaze directed at the precarious?*

It is true that I started working on precariousness philosophers in France were not really interested in this question, and there has been this interesting intersection with the work of Judith Butler. She arrived at precariousness via a very interesting reflection on the politics of crying in the experience of mourning, following the terrorist attacks of September 11[th.] What was at stake, in part, was to ask how can one be exposed to deadly violence of an unknown Other, without oneself turning to violence, continuing the cycle of death. On the other hand, she was interested in examining the conditions why only a grieved life is a life considered fully lived. Life is precarious not only in that it is exposed to the possibility of death, but also due to the possibility of not being grieved, thus appearing as a life not fully lived. From this concept of precariousness, she systematically explored social precariousness, which, in neoliberal circumstances of pitting lives in competition with one another, undoes them, and forces them to enter survivalist logic. The question of political alliance of all precarious lives, including lives made such due to their gender (LGBTQI+), presented itself to Butler as a central question: how do we come together when "we" treat ourselves as subjects already vanished or nearing the vanishing point?

My own path ran parallel to this: starting from a social understanding of precariousness, defined as social construction of a state of in-betweenness between a system of inclusion and exclusion, I came to be interested in all forms of lives situated at once within and without, including the lives of migrants, to the extent that this "within-without" is exactly the hybrid form through which precariousness is constructed. In this way, precariousness surpasses poverty and cannot be reduced to it, in the sense that extreme poverty can be characterized by the imposition of radical exclusion. An example would be the person living on the streets whose complete social belonging has been erased. By contrast, life is precarious when one of the significant social aspects of existence is unavailable (work, housing, social protection, health care, etc.). Thus, widening this intermediary zone of within-without, I have discovered that being vulnerable is precisely to be exposed to the possibility of erasure of one of the significant social aspects (including residence or state certification guaranteeing permanent access to one's society). Throughout my analysis, I pay very close attention to designations used to construct lives as "other:" "precarious," "foreigner," "unemployed," etc. These are never descriptions of immediate experience, but rather lead us to linguistic games, those that for example belong to social protection, the police station or the unemployment bureau, which themselves are in relation to hegemonic linguistic games resulting from neoliberal and ruling rationalizations. The question that presents itself is how to live with this designation, what kind of life is pushed forward by this designation, and how does life designated as other unfold, under what political, as well as anthropological conditions could the designation be removed?

The Yellow Vest movement in France not only shook the government's belief that it could forge on with reforms in an authoritarian way, it showed the central contradiction of neoliberal ideology, the necessity to return to a democracy founded on collective intelligence of the public. The popular uprising that started November 17, 2018, and which no one predicted would take place, revealed at least one truth: neoliberalism necessarily transforms electoral democracy into an authoritarian regime, which we can tell from the continuous use by the powers that be of the expressions "staying the course" and "work pedagogically,"

but also the use of the word populism in an extremely pejorative,
even contemptuous way to describe a mass primed only to be
manipulated. What does this whole context tell us about the
dominant discourse in society?

In a very interesting text from 1974, "La revolution du croyable," Michel de Certeau explains that we are in the age of the "unbelievable." Authorities rest, he says, on membership, founded on belief. Now, authorities are no longer believed. In a really prophetic way, Michel de Certeau underscores that we have become societies of escape: "What is drifting away is the sense of belonging of citizens, of parties, of unions, etc." With this escape, he says, we have entered a system of violence: "Violence occurs first of all as a rebellion against institutions and representative bodies that have become untrustworthy." I think that de Certeau understood perfectly the extent to which Exit tends to be the response to ungovernable societies. But why have societies become ungovernable? States have mutated (in the sense of a mutant) into boosters for neoliberal particles that ground our lives and render them unlivable. The refusal to be governed in this way, translated into the mobilization of the Yellow Vests, as well as other opposition associations, signifies a desire to live along entirely different mental and social coordinates. And, to refer back to de Certeau, it implies that every day our society is one of exodus, in which "those seeking to leave are more numerous than those who are nostalgic." The risk of this mass exodus is that the government remains in the hands of neoliberal conservatives who want everything to change so that nothing would change. The risk, thus, has been put well by Wendy Brown, in a completely different context: the neoliberal conservative revolution is an extreme allegiance to the laws of the market and security. How can we, in the midst of our exodus, remake society on an entirely different basis?

You have been active in numerous social movements for
democracy and freedom. Recent among these struggles was that of
the Institute for Philosophy and Social Theory in Serbia, for which
you joined the international support and which yielded positive

results. Do you think that intellectuals can make a difference in society and if so, what kind? What, in your opinion, is the role and place of intellectuals in contemporary societies and social struggles?

I believe intellectuals today are endangered just like all other instances of production and dissemination of knowledge. We are left with having to defend our positions as diagnosticians of the present, which is what intellectual activity is. In my view, it is a mistake to believe that the intellectual is set apart from concrete conditions, either social, political, or economic, which allow for the possibility of their work. There is no opposition between intellectual work and its dissemination and reception. Thus, caring for intellectuals endangered for all sorts of reasons is to care in general for institutions in which intellectual work is conducted. And these two spheres are today rather precarious: they appear as "anomalies" in a worldview, a *Weltanschauung* of profit, to which we are witness. Preserving the anomaly of intellectual work is itself the introduction of the characteristic difference between normal and pathological, between rule and exception. This means valuing the ecology of places of individuation of the world through a diagnostic critique, which are also the places of life, or better still, which indicate the forms of life. The intellectual does not necessarily create a difference, but rather follows benevolently the efforts that grow out of the ways of living that separate themselves from the neoliberal form. What is even more difficult is to call into question normativity from a standpoint that is both theoretical and practical. Here is the role of the intellectual, the creation of a separation that thinks the living separation in order to take hold of it as the production of a new communal and more desirable norm.

Interview conducted by Zona Zarić

CANNIBALISTIC CAPITALISM AND THE MEANING OF SOCIALISM IN THE TWENTY-FIRST CENTURY
Nancy Fraser

Nancy Fraser is an American philosopher and public intellectual and activist, critical theorist, feminist, professor of political and social sciences and philosophy at the New school for social research in New York City. Her main interest is in political, social and feminist theories, modern French and German philosophies. She has held positions at numerous universities (The Free university of Berlin, College d'etudes mondiales Paris, Cambridge, etc.), and is a member of the American Academy of Science and Art (2019). Her philosophical point of view is best reflected in a new critical approach to Marx, Adorno and Habermas. She studies capitalism and the consumer society, focusing on correcting maldistribution, and examining the widening inequality gap between the rich and the poor, social justice movements for recognition on the basis of race, gender, sexuality and ethnicity. Fraser emphasizes the deleterious effects of neoliberal capitalism, with regard to the development of global feminist movements and the crisis in so-called welfare states. She is author of *Unruly practices: power, discourse and gender in contemporary social theory* (1989), *Justice interrupts: critical reflections on the "post socialist" condition* (1997), *Redistribution or recognition?* (with Axel Honneth, 2003), *Scales of justice: reimagining political space in a globalising world* (2009), *Fortunes of feminism: from state-managed capitalism to neoliberal crisis* (2013), *Transnationalizing the Public Sphere* (2014), *Feminism for the 99% - a Manifesto* (2019).

Does every form of capitalist society inevitably harbor a deep-seated social-reproductive 'crisis tendency' or contradiction? And to what extent has the neoliberalization of the economy destroyed the social-democratic basis?

Capitalist society definitely has some built-in crisis tendencies, including some surrounding social reproduction. These appear not just in neoliberalism, but in every phase of capitalist development. Every phase has to deal somehow with the inherent tensions the system establishes through its constitutive division between production and reproduction. But the same is true for capitalism's deep-seated tendency to ecological crisis, which is especially acute in the current phase, but always present in capitalist society. And it is also the case for the system's structural proneness to political crisis. What this says to me is that we need to revise our understanding of capitalism. It is a relation between capital and labor, to be sure. But not only. Capitalism is also a relation between production and reproduction, society and nature, and economy and polity. So, it is not just an economic system, but a set of relations *between* its economy and the latter's background conditions of possibility – namely, carework, nature, public power. Without these "non-economic" conditions there couldn't be any production, distribution or profit.

But, here's the kicker: the way in which capitalism organizes each of these crucial relations is contradictory. Each background condition for capitalism's economy is the site of a built-in tendency to crisis. In each case, the system incentivizes capitalists to free-ride on its background conditions; it licenses them to help themselves to carework, nature, and public power, while absolving them of any responsibility for replenishing what they take or repairing what they damage. It's not an accident, therefore, that in the course of capitalism's history each of these "non-economic" supports for its economy has periodically emerged as a site of acute crisis. Throughout that history we see not only economic and financial crises, but also periodic crises of social reproduction, ecology and political governance.

Now, you asked about social democracy. That was the preferred strategy of crisis-management in the phase of state-organized capitalism, during the middle third of the 20th century. It emerged in the wealthy countries of the Global North as a response to an acute crisis of the preceding phase of liberal-colonial capitalism.

The latter had proved incapable of containing the system's built-in crisis tendencies, which burst out everywhere in the 1920s and '30s. Affecting every sphere of society and every region of the capitalist world system, this was a general crisis of the whole social order. The social-democratic "solution" was quite selective, responding to some strands of the crisis while ignoring others. Among the strands it opted to address was the social-reproduction crisis in the historic core countries of Western Europe and North America. Its strategy was to defuse that crisis by establishing state support for carework via welfare provision. Instead of allowing capital to continue cannibalizing that vital element, social-democratic governments "internalized the externality:" they brought it within the purview of state responsibility as an object of "management." The result was to stabilize the conditions of living for significant portions of the working classes in those countries and to defuse that dimension of capitalist crisis. (War production and postwar reconstruction also played major roles in restarting accumulation on an expanded scale.)

But social-democracy was a devil's bargain, involving a number of unsavory trade-offs. The gains for some came off the backs of others. Male workers' "independence" was typically built on women's dependency, as "the family wage" ideal was baked into most welfare systems. In the US, moreover, most people of color were debarred from the benefits, as agricultural and domestic labor was excluded from Social Security. Then, too, social democracy rested on an economy dominated by automobile and related manufacturing. It was effectively funded by the internal combustion engine, powered by refined oil, and by carbon-intensive consumerism, all of which vastly accelerated greenhouse gas emissions. So, this form of capitalism internalized some social reproduction costs by racking up a huge unpaid bill for ecological reproduction costs. It addressed one strand of crisis by exacerbating another one. And it offloaded many of these costs, ecological and otherwise, onto poor regions and racialized populations whose wealth was all the while being siphoned to the Global North. So social democracy was hardly a win for everyone. It involved a great deal of cost-shifting from region to region and sphere to societal sphere. All of this raises the important question of whether capitalism can handle both social-reproductive and ecological crises at once.

But of course, it's absolutely true, as you suggested, that neoliberalisation has made even that somewhat miserable trade-off impossible. It's as if the capitalists of the social-democratic era had said, "OK, we'll give you some money for social reproduction, but you have to let us spew ever more CO_2 into the atmosphere." In the neoliberal era, they're saying something else: "We're not going to give you anything – we will take it all." Neoliberalism has definitely changed the game by redrawing the balance of power between states and corporations, especially mega-corporations, and also between capital and labor, which affects social reproduction and the ecology.

But neoliberal capitalism is now itself in crisis, no longer able to contain or finesse the system's contradictions. It is cannibalizing all of its own presuppositions at once: voraciously guzzling carework, scarfing up nature, and eviscerating the public powers that could, in theory, be used to manage the crisis. So, this too is a general crisis of the whole social order, akin to that of the 1930s. It is one of those rare moments in history when all of capitalism's crisis tendencies converge. Under these conditions, it's not helpful to look at any of these crises separately, to look at the social reproductive crisis in abstraction from ecological, political, and economic crises, or vice versa. The reality is that all of these strands of our crisis complex interact with and exacerbate one another.

COVID-19 offers a textbook demonstration of these entanglements. It is a perfect storm of capitalist irrationality and injustice, in which all of the system's contradictions have come to a head. The virus itself came to us courtesy of capital, via its relentless promotion of global warming and tropical deforestation, which induced the species migrations that triggered the zoonotic transfer to us of SARS-CoV-2. We can also thank capital for a large number of the human losses, as the public capacities we could have used to mitigate them were hollowed out by forty years of neoliberal "austerity" during which public-health infrastructure was allowed to deteriorate and the lion's share of the world's treatment and research capacities were devolved to for-profit firms, unconstrained by the public interest. Capital is also to blame for the depletion of the carework capacities we have needed so badly in conditions of lockdown, as neoliberalism's low-wage regime demands increased hours of paid work per household, including from primary caregivers. And the system's ability to reckon the true worth of labor has been exposed as a fraud through the terrible spectacle of "essential" workers paid a pittance to face the dangers of infection daily in order to produce and distribute the stuff that enables others to shelter in place–a spectacle that has everything to do with capitalism's inherent dynamics of color and class.

The pandemic, then, is a perfect illustration of capitalist dysfunctionality and injustice. It reveals the inextricable intertwinement of all of the system's contradictions and crisis tendencies. We could not ask for a better lesson in critical social theory.

Your past work on the intersection and tension between redistribution and recognition (material and symbolic dimensions of domination) seems as pertinent today as it was when you first formulated it. How do you see this playing out in contemporary societies, in the US and Europe in particular?

One aspect of the current capitalist crisis is a *hegemonic* crisis, the state in which a critical mass of people now feel that the system is becoming illegitimate. This includes right-wingers like Trumpists and left-wing populists like Bernie Sanders alike – they both say "the system is rigged," but they mean quite different things by that. There is a loss of credibility in the ruling common sense that has underpinned this particular regime of capitalism. Social democracy was based on a common sense that combined redistribution and recognition within the ideal of a *family wage*, which required capital to pay the workers enough to reproduce a labor force and live a decent life. Workers could thus become full members of society, and live the "American (or Yugoslav) way of life" – there was thus both a recognition and a distribution element about what it meant to be a full member of society. In developed societies, the neoliberal dismantling of this regime happened primarily in the form of *progressive neoliberalism*, which some people might think is a contradiction in terms but I assure you it is not. In many of the most powerful nations, neoliberalisation was introduced and consolidated not by right-wing parties and governments, but by parties that called themselves socialist or Labour, or (in the case of the US) the Democratic Party, the closest we have to Labour.

These parties essentially turned the organization of economic policy over to Wall Street, which meant that they were prepared to outsource jobs, break unions, lower wages and generally gut the standard of living of the bottom two thirds of the population as long as the stock market was zooming up. The crucial tool for accomplishing this was *recognition*, which enabled progressive neoliberals to legitimize an enormous upward redistribution of wealth by being pro-feminist, pro-LGBTQ or anti-racist. They relied on a version of progressive politics of recognition which was centered not on real equality but on *meritocracy*, on letting a small number of "underrepresented" groups such as women and sexual minorities climb the corporate, military or government ladder. At the same time, progressive neoliberals were pursuing economic policies that harmed the overwhelming majority of those same people as well as the white working classes.

Progressive neoliberalism included such figures as Clinton and Obama in the US, Tony Blair in the UK, Gerhard Schröder in Germany and François Hollande in France. However, there was a breaking point in 2015/16 at which people in the US and UK began to reject this configuration – there was, on the one hand, the Sanders/Trump phenomenon, which included both right-wing and left-wing rejection of progressive neoliberalism, and on the other Brexit. The ongoing populist revolt in many countries is primarily about rejecting the progressive neoliberal way of putting together redistribution and recognition and finding another way of linking these. We could say in Gramscian terms that we are currently facing an *interregnum* in which "the old is dying and the new cannot be born."

Redistribution and recognition are not only philosophical categories for analyzing the state of (in)justice – as I argued in *Redistribution or Recognition?*, these are also *folk paradigms* of justice. They are expressions of people's basic understanding that society should have some form of a just distribution, and some sort of an appropriate recognition order in terms of who counts as a full member, who should be honored, respected and esteemed – and people might have very different ideas of what a just distribution or recognition order is. These are the building blocks for constructing hegemony and contesting it, for trying to build a counter-hegemonic bloc, and since we are in a period of a general crisis, a hegemonic as well as a structural one, it is very important to look at the redistribution and recognition trade-offs and synergies from the standpoint of constructing/deconstructing hegemony.

More recently you have been working on a theoretical program designed to expand the horizons of collective and individual freedom, of democratic citizenship. Given current conditions, where states of exception are becoming the norm, could you tell us what the conditions would be to move towards reimagined social-democratic societies?

This again relates to the present crisis of capitalism, since there is a whole set of structural injustices built into the capitalist system. The exact form these injustices take in different periods, countries and regimes will vary. Since there is a tendency to a social-reproductive crisis in any form of capitalism, there is also a tendency to gender asymmetry and male domination. In the same way, there is a tendency to racial imperial domination and oppression because of the built-in tension between the *exploited* and *expropriated* labor. Exploitation, as seen from the Marxian perspective, means that workers are supposed to receive in wages the living cost – however, wage labor in capitalism in terms of formal contract has actually accounted for only a small portion of the global labor that is done to keep the world going, and so we have the unwaged carework labor, a huge amount of unfree or dependent labor, informal gray- and black-market labor and trafficked labor.

One dimension of the *ecological crisis*, therefore, is the expropriation of the wealth and natural resources of the lands of peripheralized peoples, as in the idea that the social democracy of the rich rests in the expropriation of the poor. The relation between expropriation and exploitation is complicated, but it roughly corresponds to the global "color line" – this line divides the populations that are merely exploited from those that are brutally expropriated, and that is a structural difference in capitalism. Contrary to the apologists of capitalism, expropriation is necessary to make exploitation profitable. As many figures from Rosa Luxemburg to David Harvey have insisted, there is a built-in set of structurally undergirded forms of racial and imperial oppression in capitalism, even indigenous dispossession and genocide. The forms of wealth drain and land grabs happening today are quite different from those in the era of racial chattel slavery in the New World, but these are both forms of expropriation that are articulated with, and underpinned by, a system of exploitation.

Capitalism has, built into it, not just the standard socialist problem of class domination but structurally entrenched gender, racial, ethnic and imperial asymmetries. There is an inherent tendency in capitalism towards hollowing out democracy, which is due to the fact that this system rests on a division between public and private power. The public power is responsible for taking care of the army, the law and decision making on some issues, and private power (capitalists) are supposed to take care of production, the organization of energy and the food system. Capitalism is thus creating a class of people who have considerable power and a built-in incentive to evade taxes, weaken regulations, capture regulatory agencies, privatize public goods and generally weaken public powers. The present conditions of defanged, weakened citizenship rights and democratic freedom are not a free-standing political problem which could be solved by redesigning the political system – these are the very conditions under which the above tendencies of capitalism become acute. We have to re-imagine the relation between the economy and polity, and to re-manage the relation between production and reproduction, between society and nature.

In the US, there is now a lot of shallow talk of "bipartisanship" and "civility" – what we really need to reflect on is how to reorganize the relation between the public and private power, because states have systematically been deprived of the tools in their toolkit which they used to have, in the social-democratic era, to make corporations pay taxes or reign in their polluting. There has been a systematic shift in the relation between public and corporate power to the detriment of the former. You can't fix this problem without doing something about capital and corporations and their place in the world – whether that means abolishing them completely or finding some new way of organizing them. But we can't talk about the problem of democracy without talking about the problem of capitalism.

In line with all this, how do you envisage reestablishing the notion of the common good in societies where neoliberal policies have generated deep seated anomie and atomization? What are the possible pathways towards the dialectical enhancement of individual and collective freedoms?

In a society that is systematically organized around class domination, gender asymmetry and racial oppression, the appeal to the common good is a sham. What we need to be thinking about is the question of *power*, of how to organize some sort of powerful broad alliance of social forces that can generate enough counter-power to force a change in the institutional framework and structure of society. I keep coming back to the idea of a *counter-hegemonic bloc* – there is now a wide array of impressively creative and courageous social movements, but the overall landscape is fragmented, these do not add up yet to a real counter-hegemonic force with a shared vision, in which the whole question of democratic freedom and community would have to be a central part along with an ecological policy to stop global warming. We are dealing with problems that are so deeply rooted in our form of social organization that their solution requires a deep structural change in the form of social organization, and this requires a very powerful alliance of forces who would have to come to see that, different as the problems and situations they experience are, the roots of the experienced problems all point to the same thing.

Such an understanding could be the basis for a large counter-hegemonic alliance or project. This alliance would have to look very different from what socialist or communist movements looked like in the past, because these were primarily "workerist," too much focused on factory workers – the latter are an important aspect, but the nature of the 21st century society involves a proliferation of a whole variety of different forms of service work, which means that there are new actors. It is a more complicated job today to create a common sense of a counter-hegemonic project, but there will have to be ideas about redistribution, recognition and democratization. A classic problem in socialist theory has always been how to combine democratic participation with socialist planning. I believe, contrary to the anarchist left that a lot of my students are drawn to, that there is no solution to so many of our mega-problems (such as COVID-19) that does not involve considerable coordination and planning on a transnational and global scale. Those are the kinds of questions that begin to get at what is needed in order to expand the horizons of collective and individual freedom and overcome anomie and atomization.

The ongoing pandemic has, through its foregrounding of the value of science, sparked a certain revival of the traditional left's scientism, underpinned by such notions as "Reason" and "Truth" in the Enlightenment sense. This revival occurs in the context of the ascent of right-wing populism and the question of how to fight the onslaught of "post-truth" mentality and its techniques of government and political mobilization exemplified by fake news, "alternative facts" and conspiracy theories. In light of your distrust of foundationalism, how would you respond to the scientistic tendencies on the left and what would be an adequate strategy for combating the political techniques of the right?

You are right that I am an anti-foundationalist at the level of epistemology, but for me that does not translate into any suspicion of science. The most important way to combat the political techniques of the right has nothing to do with defending science. It has to do with fighting for policies that can improve peoples' lives. I'm not saying that bad lives lead in a straight line to conspiracy thinking, but there is some relation. Part of the problem with progressive neoliberalism is that it includes a constant danger of condescending to the poor, left-behind people who believe all sorts of nasty things – progressive neoliberals tend to put on a face of rationality, which antagonizes people. I want to understand the ways in which these people are victims. In the US context, I am not talking about the Proud Boys, extreme militias and white supremacists. These are lost, I'm not trying to reason with them. But they are different from "ordinary MAGA" (Make America Great Again) people. Some ordinary MAGA people are reachable, indeed they have to be – we can't start out thinking they are hopeless. In order to reach them, we should develop a social movement that fights for their interests as we understand them, and that we think will make their lives better.

The impressive number of votes for Trump in the US presidential elections and other recent developments around the world seem to suggest that disadvantaged social groups still misunderstand the real causes of their deprivation, mistaking economic causes of deprivation for "cultural" ones. Despite the general re-legitimization of redistributive politics in the aftermath of the 2008 crisis, the language of recognition politics (or of "culture wars" as is nowadays fashionable) still seems to have a capacity to displace the vocabulary of economic justice as a toolbox that people use to make sense of their grievances. How do you explain this persistent dominance of the recognition paradigm – why do people turn to Trump and not to Sanders?

People turned to Trump because the Clinton wing of the Democratic Party essentially shut down the Bernie Sanders campaign. The progressive neoliberals used every tool they had to attack the left, we saw that not only in 2016 but also in 2020. You have to understand that the left has more than one opponent to deal with at the same time. It seemed to me that the Obama-Clinton wing of the Democratic Party would rather lose the election to Trump than empower Sanders. Then you have Trump himself, and this is the hard thing to understand – he is a kind of genius propagandist. Even those who hate him can't stop watching him. All these leaders – Erdogan, Putin, Modi, Bolsonaro – have powerful auras of some kind, different in each case. We need a kind of mass psychology perspective to understand the cathexis that binds people to these figures.

Would it also be right to say, since you mentioned Gramsci, that there are some structural underlying reasons for the populist success which have to do with hegemony – for example that the right has to some extent successfully created a "chain of equivalence" between progressive neoliberalism and the left?

That's exactly what I would say – and the populists didn't do it out of thin air. They managed to do this because progressive neoliberalism laid the groundwork, created the appearance that feminism was an elite thing for selfish career women, because that's the kind of feminism progressive neoliberals supported. They created a whole set of policies that, instead of addressing the changes in the society that were harming both the black and the white working class even if the forms of harm were different, developed a superficial recognition politics that did nothing for white workers. The links that the right-wing populists and demagogues build on were put in place (or at least the possibility to make those links) by progressive neoliberalism's little scam with redistribution and recognition.

You recently argued, in a Rortian spirit, that we are currently going through an intense period of "abnormal justice", a condition in which a relative consensus regarding the legitimate agents of justice claims and the physical and conceptual space of possible justice claims breaks down. Is the condition of abnormal justice a more favorable setting for a transformationist political agenda,

*in the sense that the normative and symbolic indeterminacy it
creates opens up greater space for social actors to "redescribe"
themselves more radically?*

Yes, for good and for ill. People can redescribe themselves in a
fascist way or in a socialist emancipatory way. The point is that,
historically speaking, the political space is not uniform, gradual
and linear. I understand the history of modern, capitalist societies
through a kind of Rortian or Kuhnian perspective: there are periods
of relative stability in which there is a guiding paradigm or a
common sense – this does not mean there is total agreement, but the
dissent is contained within certain limits, or marginalized. That's
the period of "normal politics" in which people agree, more or less,
on the rules of the game and then fight for better positions within
the game as it is defined. But then we have periods of abnormality,
or revolutionary periods in Kuhnian language (or interregnum in
Gramscian language). These abnormalities are always describing a
situation of betweenness, where you don't have anything like the
normal level of agreement on what you can disagree about. I use the
metaphor of the "wilding" of public space, in which there are many
more totally out-of-the-box ideas that would have had no take-up in
a normal period but can get a hearing now.

So, we are witnessing a certain speeding up of people's self-
redescription, but what is good for the goose is good for the gander,
it works for the right as well. I do think that people are now open to
ideas that represent a more radical break with the status quo – it's
partially because they have less to lose. In normal times, people
have to weigh – to the extent that they are being calculative and
instrumental – the trade-off between fighting for something big
and losing (and therefore losing something) or making baby steps
and having a better chance of winning. Those are hard choices. In
a situation like ours, things are not working for so many people
that there's a sense of having less to lose. That's why I think this is
the moment when the left should be thinking big.

*Finally, you have been active in many initiatives fighting for
democracy and freedom. One of those was for the Institute for*

Philosophy and Social Theory in Belgrade where you joined the call for support and became a member of our International Academic Committee. Do you believe that intellectuals can make a difference and if so, what kind?

There are many different kinds of intellectuals – climate scientists have made a difference, and so have Noam Chomsky and Edward Snowden, for example. I'm an academic, a critical theorist and a philosopher by training and, personally, I'm trying to write in a way that is rigorous enough to meet my relatively high standards and at the same time speak to a somewhat broader audience. So, I think of myself as a kind of "relay point" between academia and social movements. In my personal case, that's because I came out of the New Left, I was an activist before I was an academic and my position in academia always involved juggling with these tensions. Right now, for all the reasons that we've been discussing – the hegemonic crisis, the seriousness of the ecological crisis, the openings and the dangers, the re-emergence in the United States of something closer to "the left" than we had before – I am beginning to feel young again, prepared to take risks and be bolder, and that probably shows in my most recent writings.

People are now more willing to listen to out-of-the-box ideas, and I hope this also means that intellectuals are willing to think such ideas and put them out there. Intellectuals can be spark plugs – it's not a one-way street, we get a lot of our best ideas by reflecting on what people are doing in the streets. What I think I can do is help systematize some of the very good ideas that are in the air at this moment. I wrote a paper "What Should Socialism Mean in the 21st Century" because I was inspired by everybody talking about socialism lately, which is an extraordinary thing. This is an example of what an intellectual can do in this situation – as well as signing, lending whatever value your name has as an intellectual in support of good causes and people who need support, like your Institute.

Interview conducted by Zona Zarić and Marjan Ivković

POWER, PROFIT AND PRESTIGE:
ON AMERICAN AND CHINESE IMPERIALISM
Philip Golub

Philip Golub is an American and French political scientist. Professor of Political Science, Political Philosophy and International Relations at the American University of Paris (AUP), he has taught at the Institute of European Studies, University of Paris 8, and in the graduate program of Sciences-Po Paris. His research focuses on the state, globalization, and late-modern and contemporary international imperial history, as well as contemporary civil society's problems, diplomacy and international law. He is the author of numerous studies and publications, focusing on Asian political economy, as well as dozens of book chapters on various issue areas of world politics. He is also a prolific author and commentator in the press and audiovisual media. He has published several books: *East Asia's Reemergence* (2016), *Power, Profit and Prestige: A History of American Imperial Expansion* (2010), *Une autre histoire de la puissance américaine* (2015).

You are the author of a very interesting and impressive book entitled Power, Profit and Prestige: A History of American Imperial Expansion, *in which you present a synthetic 'alternative' history of the United States. Perhaps the best-known alternative history of the United States was written by Howard Zinn in* A People's History of the United States. *What do you think about this book and its author? It seems to us that your two books are quite complementary: your focus is more on the macro perspective and Howard Zinn's is more on the micro. How do you see the connection between these two books?*

PPP, as I like to call the book, is a historical-sociological study of the material and ideational forces involved in the United States' emergence as the core state of the world capitalist economy. It situates U.S. ascent in the wider context of the Industrial Revolution and Eurocentric globalization, arguing that the country's nineteenth century territorial and economic expansion was an integral and dynamic part of these broader systemic transformations. At the same time, it takes a close and hard look at the imperial cosmologies – the set of assumptions about historical purpose and cultural and racial hierarchy – that became the matrix of elite visions of world order. Identifying regularities over time, I show that empire became the habitus of dominant U.S. social groups, just as in Europe where it constitutes a past that has never really passed. This focus on global power logics differs from Zinn's work, which primarily looks at domestic social struggles and aims to give narrative voice to the vulnerable and persecuted. Both deal with power, domination and violence however, and can be read as part of the broader critical social studies movement that took off in the 1960s and that challenged mainstream Eurocentric historical and cultural narratives, opening new vistas for critical research on the dark sides of western modernity: empire, coloniality, and problems of gender, race and class.

Could you describe the historical dynamic that has allowed the United States to move, in just a century and a half, from being a former British colony to being an economic, military and cultural superpower surpassing Europe and becoming a hyper-power, to quote Hubert Védrine, or perhaps the greatest world power thus far?

Broadly speaking, one can distinguish between an initial developmental phase driven by U.S. insertion in a rapidly expanding transatlantic economic system, a second phase of continental integration and intense industrialization in the late nineteenth and the early twentieth centuries, and the phase of global ascent during and after the Second World War when the US supplanted western Europe at the center and the apex. In the first, US economic development and territorial expansion in a continent with vast natural resources were driven by the transnational linkages of the Atlantic world. British economic expansion and U.S. expansion were part of a symbiotic development dynamic structured around slave labor, international commodity chains, and transnational capital flows. Already in the latter part of the eighteenth century, the Mainland American colonies had become a vital hub in the transnational linkages of the "Atlantic World," in which constantly rising British demand transformed the US into the predominant New World exporter of colonial goods (sugar, tobacco and cotton primarily). Transatlantic trade rose continuously through the colonial era down to the War of Independence and greatly prospered in the first half of the nineteenth century. The future United States' share of total exports from the Americas rose from 0.02 per cent in 1650, to 22.2 per cent in 1800 to just over 56 per cent in the mid-nineteenth century.

Most of the increase from the early 1800s on was attributable to cotton, the pacemaker of industrial change during the first Industrial Revolution in Britain, hence on slave labor. While the plantations in the West Indies had been Britain's primary source of sugar and raw cotton until in the 1790s, the British textile industry – the first globalized industry – "acquired a new and virtually unlimited source in the slave plantations of the Southern USA" (Hobsbawm). Before the Civil War (1861-5) the U.S. accounted for more than two thirds of world cotton output. The U.S. South, in Adam Rothman's words, became the "leading edge of a dynamic, expansive slave regime incorporated politically into the United States and firmly tied to the transatlantic system of commodity exchange." This system not only created vast riches for the southern planters but also promoted capital accumulation in the northern states, which served as the hubs of the United States' international trade and were the center of the country's own textile industry. Northern merchants were the intermediaries of transatlantic commerce and U.S. firms built a significant proportion of the ships which carried the trade. Financing came from Britain and northern U.S. financial institutions: New York City emerged as America's economic capital due to its role in financing and structuring the transatlantic cotton trade.

The second phase after the Civil War involved the constitution of an integrated continental market, of which the industrializing north was the dynamic core, as the U.S. completed its expansion and established its sovereignty "from sea to sea." The upper Midwest become incorporated into the rapidly developing eastern industrial economy, a process that was favored by continuing capital flows, notably from Britain which invested most of its surpluses in the U.S. and the colonies of settlement (from the end of the Civil War to 1900, the share of investment flowing to the United States averaged 22 per cent of total British sourced investment in the world). It was also crucially favored by transnational migrations that played a decisive role in industrialization and urbanization in the latter part of the century, creating a vast pool of low-cost wage-seeking labor for the expanding post-bellum north-eastern and north-western industrial economy, which was protected from foreign competition by consistently high tariffs. From 1860 to 1920, the ratio of immigrants to total population averaged 13-14 per cent but was significantly higher as a share of the total workforce (20% in 1900). More than 33 million immigrants moved to the United States between 1820 and 1924. Without them, according to some estimates, the current population of the United States would be one third less...

Europe was thus the unconscious accomplice of the US' rise in the nineteenth century, even more so during the two general wars in the first half of the twentieth. In the 1890s, the U.S. had already become the world's leading industrial power. By 1914, it accounted for 23.5% of world manufacturing output (Britain, 18.5%; Germany, 13.5%, France, 6%), a share that rose to around 39% just prior to the Great Depression (31% during the early 1930s). During and after the Great War, New York gained prominence as an international financial center, and the dollar became an increasingly important instrument of international payments. Just as the U.S. relied on British finance in the nineteenth century (it is noteworthy that the U.S. raised funds for its war of conquest against Mexico in 1846-48 in the City of London), Britain became dependent on U.S. capital to finance the European war.

During the Second World War, the U.S. became the industrial "workshop of the world" and its technological leader: the economy grew by nearly 50% while continental Europe and East Asia were being devastated. In 1945, the U.S. accounted for nearly half of world output and world trade and had become the world's sole creditor. It had obtained planetary strategic reach, and established hegemonic (in the Gramscian sense) alliance systems in western Europe and East Asia that proved lasting during and indeed after the Cold War. Despite much talk of U.S. decline during the 1970s and 80s, the collapse of the Soviet State and the dissolution of the USSR in 1991 revealed structural asymmetries that had long favored the United States. In the decade and a half following that "quiet cataclysm," the U.S. enjoyed a brief moment of global predominance. Today, China's reemergence and its growing role in the capitalist world economy has fundamentally altered this configuration.

We often hear that we are heading towards a multipolar world, and that we will no longer have a dominant power that will impose on the rest of the world disciplinary rules of the game. You question the notion of multipolarity, so how do you see this?

I do my best to avoid the impoverished language and conceptual aridity of "geopolitics," and am impatient with deterministic realist International Relations frameworks that reduce world politics to a kind of blind and timeless Newtonian mechanics. I am also deeply skeptical of formalized models of "great power" rises and falls according to cycles and supposed "laws" of historical motion (Modelski, Kondratieff, etc.). My analytical concern is to develop genetic accounts of change that are sensitive to the dialectic of structure, agency, and contingency.

The systemic change we are now witnessing should be situated in long historical perspective. The early-modern world was characterized by coincident regional evolutions where parts of the Ottoman Empire, South Asia, China, Southeast Asia and Europe were simultaneously engaged in "industrious revolutions", with expanding commercial cultures. In Europe, as Braudel elegantly shows, maritime city-states took turns in being cores of transcontinental commerce, knowledge, craftmanship, finance and the arts. These hubs of early modern globalization, surrounded by backward continental hinterlands, connected Europe to other hubs in Asia and the Middle East through long distance trade.

The Industrial Revolution and Eurocentric imperial globalization broke this plural pattern, leading to an exceptional concentration of wealth and power in the north Atlantic "West," and to the division of the world into dominant cores and colonial peripheries. Great Britain, the epicenter of the Industrial Revolution, was the leading though not the sole actor in this hierarchical reordering that generated new and lasting structures of international inequality. For a time, Europe set global rules and regimes, and "modernity" became inextricably bound to coloniality. The U.S., as I indicated in my earlier remarks, was an integral component in this general phenomenon. The non-territorial empire that emerged in 1945, founded on the country's structural power as the gravitational center of the capitalist political economy, reproduced some of the features of the European era (disciplinary "interventions" in the postcolonial world) but innovated by legitimating its rule-making through institutions (World Bank, IMF, NATO, etc.) that put power asymmetries in the background, preserving the fiction of *de jure* equality but effectively codifying hierarchy.

This long era of Euro-Atlantic predominance is coming to an end. The current process of East-West rebalancing means that significant parts, though not all, of the "peripheries" have broken out or are breaking out of the constraints that until relatively recently inhibited international upward mobility and economic-technological convergence with the most advanced economies of the "North." East Asia's reemergence marks the beginning of a new sequence of world politics in which the world will revolve once more around plural if interdependent centers of gravity.

The systemic transformation of which you speak is taking place within the capitalist system itself. China is a capitalist country, whose capitalism is more brutal than that of the countries of contemporary Western Europe, but her development invalidates the neoliberal thesis in the sense that its extraordinary growth has been due mainly to state intervention and planning. What does the fact that China and the United States are capitalist powers change in terms of their rivalry compared to the US-Soviet rivalry?

Students of the Industrial Revolution and of the rise of modern capitalism have long questioned why China, with its rich early modern history of scientific-technical innovations, had not made the leap from industrious to industrial revolution. One influential but deeply flawed answer was that the weight of cultural factors (Confucianism and its institutional effects) inhibited the development and application of systematic scientific knowledge, blocking the rationalization process that led to the diffusion of modern capitalism in northern Europe and its settler colonial offshoots. "Why the West" and "why not China" became interlinked questions in a narrative that pointed to a supposed European cultural singularity. Weber's Protestant Ethic was the earliest and most sophisticated expression of this line of thought, spawning later modernization theorists (Parsons, Eisenstadt, Bellah and Rostow…) and, in a decaying intellectual trajectory, their heirs (Huntington, David Landes, Niall Ferguson, etc.). For all his Eurocentrism, Marx proved more perspicacious and prescient when he argued that the globalization of capitalism would pull Asia out of what he dismissively called the "idiocy of rural life," leading to a transition from "the "village system" to industrial modernity and hence, in his theory of history, to socialism. He was right on the first point but not on the second: China moved from Maoism to State capitalism, with world transforming consequences.

China's gradual and willful integration into the world capitalist economy in the 1980s and 1990s was carefully steered by the State, the policies of which were largely modelled on precursor East Asian developmental states (Japan, South Korea, Taiwan, Singapore). Foreign investment flows from regional capital then from the world served to build endogenous manufacturing capacity and, more importantly, to give Chinese firms and technicians access to know-how and technology. China became a manufacturing platform, initially for low valued-added export products, then for more sophisticated and higher value-added ones. Opening and internationalization was enthusiastically supported by transnational firms who were seeking comparative advantages (cheap disciplined labor) across the globe as part of the restructuring of capitalism. It was also encouraged by the United States, which assumed that economic liberalization, besides benefiting western firms, would bring China into conformity with the disciplines of the western-centered world order and gradually shift its domestic political order. This hasn't happened, of course: authoritarianism has gone hand in hand with capitalist transformation, invalidating the tenacious liberal assumption that democracy and capitalism were/are synonymous.

The USSR, in contrast, shut itself off from the capitalist world economy, and was firmly kept out through the West's containment policies. By the late 1970s, the Soviet economy was exhibiting signs of sharp economic decline that became unmanageable and ultimately led to state collapse. Perestroika and Glasnost were too little too late. China chose a path of domestic economic liberalization and international integration to save the Party-state system, which maintained a tight repressive grip on politics (Tiananmen). Despite foreign market and technology dependencies and concerns over "technology-less" industrialization, the PRC managed to move upwards in the global value chain (I discuss this in detail East Asia's Reemergence). Since the late 2000s China has become an "active unit" of the world capitalist system "whose program is not simply adapted to its environment but which adapts the environment to its program" (to borrow a concept that François Perroux uses in other contexts). Multisectoral industrial policies since the 2000s, strategic investments in R&D, and continuing large scale capital inflows into mid and high-tech sectors have made the country into a major technological power, with some key sectors at or near the technological frontier. This has strategic implications, through a significant and sustained buildup and upgrading of the Chinese armed forces.

For the U.S., as well as many countries in Asia that now live in China's shadow, China has become too rich, too powerful, too quick. China for its part sees the U.S., which since 1945 dominated the regional political economy, as a potential threat. Despite deep economic interdependencies, strategic tensions have been sharpening over growing Chinese assertiveness over Taiwan, Hong Kong, and the South China Sea, its handling of the COVID pandemic, and the dramatic domestic repression of the Uighurs. The U.S. has been taking measures to decouple, to curb Chinese access to essential technologies and to block Chinese investment. So, the risk of shocks is rising, all the more so that nationalist circles in both the U.S. and China read the current competition in oppositional cultural terms. Chinese scholars close to the regime have revived the neo-Weberian cultural paradigm and turned it on its head, arguing that China's modernization is rooted in the Confucianism ethic (that Mao dubbed "feudal junk"), counterposing "Asian values" (said to be the acceptance of social hierarchy, top-down authority and thrift) to Western "decadence." On the other side of the Pacific, Huntington's performative idea of a "clash of civilizations" is never far from the surface. Cultural essentialization is highly flammable stuff…

One last thought on this: from a standpoint of global justice, rebalancing is a good since it redresses historically constructed inequalities. It corresponds to the historic aims of generations of anticolonial leaders and critical thinkers who sought de jure and de facto equality in a fairer world system. Yet unlike the forward-looking voices who sought to invent a "third way" between capitalism and communism, and to make independence rhyme with social progress, the actors of the current shift are claiming a central competitive place in the capitalist world system that their predecessors had attempted either to reform or supplant. The success of that claim, in China in particular, has entirely submerged the broader emancipatory or universalistic dimensions of the long struggle for independence, equality, and social justice. The poverty of imagination of current Western leaders is mirrored by the poverty of philosophy of their postcolonial southern and eastern counterparts, who with very few exceptions lack a positive idea of what Arturo Escobar has called "an alternative ordering of the real."

In your opinion, how likely is it that the current pandemic will change the power balance between the global powers? Are we going to have the geopolitical winners and losers of this crisis at its end?

The pandemic has brought to light the deeply problematic character of global free trade and investment regimes, in two ways. First, it revealed the perilous vulnerabilities induced by acute dependence on China for medical equipment and medicines, and on other countries such as India for vaccine production. These dependencies flow from the decades-long global redeployment of manufacturing by transnational pharmaceutical firms ("big pharma"). Second, it has underlined the ethical scandal of the international property rights regime (TRIPS), enforced by the U.S. and E.U., that governs the production and distribution of goods essential to public health. It is hard to find strong enough words to qualify the choice by the U.S. and E.U. to block the demand by 80 developing countries in early March 2021 to waive the patent rights of global firms on COVID-19 vaccine production for poorer countries. The essential questions, then, are how to reduce vulnerabilities and create a fair global regime that adheres to the idea that health is a global public good.

Would you call yourself an engaged intellectual? Or is that a pleonasm? In the same way that public intellectual is a pleonasm, because shouldn't an intellectual necessarily be publicly engaged?

I consider myself a critical social theorist, in the sense initially given to that term by the Frankfurt School or kin perspectives that strive for the rigorous production of knowledges that advance what Horkheimer called "emancipation," or the expansion of the frontiers of individual and collective self-determination to "satisfy the needs and powers of human beings." Another way of putting this is to say that critical social theory is geared towards discovering the force fields, the structural conditions and mechanisms that generate various forms of material and symbolic domination, the power asymmetries within and across societies that inhibit freedom, and to mobilize these discoveries for emancipatory purposes. This normative moral philosophical and political philosophical commitment lies in the background but is never absent from rigorous research which serves a critical function in itself by bringing to light the logics of social being and social action that are not accessible through simple intuition or immediate perception since they are buried in the structures, the "unconscious" of social order.

This intellectual positioning assumes that we make judgments and interpretations that modify the facts on which they are passed, and that "enter into the actual constitution or production" of the social world. It can be considered a form of "engagement," though not of the Sartrean type, opening pathways of resistance and potential change. It implies a choice of research objects and teaching subjects that touch on problems of domination. In my case: the legacies of empire, the material and symbolic faces of power, and of course socio-economic inequality. That choice contains a normative commitment to greater equality, social justice, self-determination, and the common good – a commitment that is brought to the public arena.

As I have noted in other locations, direct engagement raises issues distinct from the epistemological and methodological problems of social enquiry, but the scholar is perforce also a citizen who cannot escape the question of moral choice, being inevitably swept up in the historical currents, the struggles and ethical dilemmas of the present. Coming from a family of painters, I see analogies between the scholar and the artist. The pen, like the brush, can generate new meanings or sensibilities that become appropriated and reinterpreted by readers and listeners and give them "reasons to act" (to borrow the name of a famous book collection founded by Pierre Bourdieu).

Finally, you have been active in many initiatives fighting for democracy and freedom. For instance, you signed a petition with Pierre Bourdieu in 1999 against the bombing of Belgrade. The latest one was for the Serbian Institute for Philosophy and Social Theory, where you joined the international call for support that brought some positive results. Do you believe that intellectuals can make a difference and if so, what kind?

My public engagements of this type have not been limited to Serbia, though I am indeed proud to have contributed to defending the Institute for Philosophy and Social Theory! Do intellectuals make a difference? In this case yes, since the petition bringing together a broad array of thinkers positively influenced the result. Zola made a difference, because of the moral power and prestige of his "*J'accuse*". In other cases, such as wars and large-scale conflicts, far less or none at all. One simple example, we were very many to oppose the invasion of Iraq in 2003, from different horizons and perspectives, to no effect. So, it's very contextual, dependent on the historic circumstances surrounding this kind of direct engagement. While considering these interventions a kind of moral requirement, I think the more profound way intellectuals shape society and history is when new constellations of ideas arise that generate new understandings of what is and what should be, new normative frontiers that then diffuse more widely in society.

Interview conducted by Zona Zarić and Ivica Mladenović

THE CRISIS OF SOCIAL DEMOCRACY IS JUST THE LATEST IN A SERIES OF LEFT-WING DEFEATS

Gáspár Miklós Tamás

Gáspár Miklós Tamás[1] was a Hungarian Marxist philosopher, public intellectual and publicist, known as one of Europe's most emblematic leftist intellectuals. He was a vocal opponent at the time of Hungarian "real socialism," and more recently of the Hungarian government led by Viktor Orbán and the Fidesz party, but also of capitalism in general. He was also politically involved as president of the Green Left in Hungary. In addition to being a regular lecturer in the region (ELTE, CEU, Babe□-Bolyai), he taught at many universities in the anglophone world, such as Oxford University, University of Chicago, Georgetown, Yale, and Columbia. He was Director of the Institute of Philosophy of the Hungarian Academy of Sciences. Until shortly before his death, he was a regular contributor to *Mérce* and *OpenDemocracy*, where he wrote primarily about political and aesthetic questions. He served in the Hungarian Parliament as a representative of the Alliance of Free Democrats (SZDSZ) from 1989 to 1994. In the early years of the 21st century, he began re-identifying as Marxist. After 2011, Tamás became a regular guest and friend of the Institute for Philosophy and Social Theory.

---

1   In the time that it took to prepare the English edition of this book, our friend and comrade, Gáspár Miklós Tamás sadly passed away. Given his ruthless criticism of various regimes under which he lived and his utter refusal to keep silent about ways to struggle for a better world, he is perhaps the very embodiment of the engaged intellectual. We would like to think, therefore, that his words in this interview, given towards the end of his life, take on an even stronger meaning and greater poignancy.

*The cooperation between Aleksandar Vučić and Viktor Orbán
has been intense for years. What do you think about this and the
common features of these regimes?*

The various Eastern European regimes, despite their differences,
are similar in that "real socialism" was the last rational state which
they can recall. The planned economy, the redistributive state that
had effects on all segments of society, the Party that preserved
and limited the system's identity, equality and mobility, the
paternalistic, caring administration, the industrializing-urbanizing
development that cultivated the people, the civilizational structure
that ensured the primacy of high culture did not satisfy the
modernizing (mainly consumerist) desires of the system, but it
had a solid outline and had arguments – authoritarian, of course
– for discipline and stability. In Yugoslavia, this was reinforced
by an anti-fascist mythology, anti-Stalinism and a federalist-
antinationalist state ideology that was lacking elsewhere. The
collapse of the last known order is a history of decline in the eyes
of the peoples of Eastern Europe.

Of all the post-1989 state practices, only ethnicism is successful,
the market-competitive capitalism based on private property is
as unpopular as the worldview of human rights, liberties, civil
society, pluralism, etc. Economic interest and the power of the
upper class fused with politics seem to be the only realities, even
though they are surrounded by hatred.

There is little to hold society together except the suspicion
of this or that 'outside': but it is not only Muslims or Russians
(in Poland and Romania) or the European Union (in the Czech
Republic or on the Hungarian right) who are seen as the enemy,
but also the domestic political opponent. These are societies
without binders, in which the background to dictatorial aspirations
is not dumb obedience but chaos, decay, especially the bankruptcy
of state administration, including infrastructure and social policy.

*You joined the international call for solidarity with the Institute
for Philosophy and Social Theory in Belgrade; and for several*

years you have been voicing your opposition to the repression of educational and scientific institutions in Hungary (CEU, MTA, University of Theatre and Film Arts, etc.). While our Institute has changed the composition of its Board of Directors and elected a new director, the struggle for Hungarian institutions seem to have failed. Is it possible that all this happened because Serbia is not yet a member of the European Union? I also ask this because you recently published an article about how the EU is actually indifferent to Orbán's political actions – in Hungary.

The European Union is not a federation that could impose a common constitutional order; the hypothesis that states with similar constitutional systems would voluntarily unite in it has been proven wrong: the countries of Central and Eastern Europe are not liberal democracies and are not well-ordered states; this cannot be said of the Visegrád Four, nor of Slovenia, Bulgaria or Romania (although there are significant differences between them), nor of Serbia, Albania, Macedonia or Kosovo. None of the former 'socialist' countries is consolidated, all lack important liberties and guarantees, all have staggering levels of social injustice, all citizens are fleeing to the West. Whether they are members of the EU or not. Meanwhile, in Western European countries, the compromise made between 1945 and 1989 is wavering. Important and recently strong countries such as Britain, France and Italy are in turmoil. Solidarity between EU members, if it ever existed, has disappeared. We see nothing but primitive selfishness. The balance that existed during the Cold War has been lost, and Europe could not replace it with something else.

You also supported the 2012 student movement protests in Hungary. I remember one of your articles that suggested that the reference to university autonomy is very problematic. Could you elaborate on that?

The autonomy of the university – or of cultural institutions – (and of course of non-elected institutions such as the courts or the central bank) is of course not democratic and not egalitarian, but a privilege. So is the autonomy of the market, where competition is regulated, but it is regulated anarchy, where the losers are not compensated. I am not a fan of elitism. Unfortunately, however, in the current circumstances, where all forms of freedom are under threat, we must be more cautious, and even defend the autonomy of the institutions of the elite against the duality of dictatorship and chaos. If the privileges of the cultural elite are the last remaining spaces of free speech, our leftist opposition to elitism is not timely at the moment, because it would only support dictatorial ambitions. So, we should rather try to extend and spread privileges by creating self-management institutions (strong trade unions in the first place) in other spheres, which at the moment seems like a hopeless utopia.

In many countries, the corona virus has brought with it the phenomena of authoritarianism and securitization. Did something similar happen in Hungary?

Nothing of the sort. Measures against the corona virus have been implemented by a broad consensus, apart from justified technical criticisms. The Orbán government used this as an excuse to introduce authoritarian measures, which were then half withdrawn, but which it continues to introduce, with varying degrees of effectiveness. The liquidation of public property among the 'deep state' power groups continues, the further impoverishment of the underclass and the precariat continues, racism and fascist ideological propaganda continue to dominate the central media, whether there is an epidemic or not.

You wrote several articles on what you called post-fascism, comparing the different manifestations of this ideology. How do you view the current protests in the US, particularly Black Lives Matter? Can parallels be drawn with what has happened in Europe in recent years?

The anti-racist wave has already swept across the Atlantic. Although it does not target the state itself (it is not a revolutionary movement), like the anti-globalist and ecological movements, it is extremely violent and impassioned, driven by moral indignation. I think it is very nice that one of the oppressive societies – because they all are! – is at least partly ashamed of its terrible past and present and is trying to mend its ways. I find it hypocritical to complain about certain excesses and acts of violence, which misses the moral point. Unfortunately, European criticism of BLM reeks of racism. Every moral revolution destroys as well as builds, and anyone who fails to see this is suffering from historical blindness. When the black equality movement arrived in Europe, we had already gone through the racist turnaround of the refugee crisis, which had fatally poisoned the public life of every European state. The dark reality of Europe, whose existence was revealed by the war in Yugoslavia, is determining the nature of politics not only in the Balkans, but throughout Europe. Two centuries have passed since the French Revolution and the idea of equality is meeting with as much, if not more, resistance than it did in the feudal systems of the $18^{\text{th century}}$.

Not only socialist but also bourgeois achievements are under threat. It is no use sympathizing with blacks in America if we persecute and oppress Muslims and Gypsies, if the Orthodox hate Catholics and vice versa, if we excuse mass murders committed by our own ethnic group and condemn those of others.

In this respect, the task has not changed for centuries – and is not being fulfilled.

Today you are one of the most prominent intellectuals on the left. How do you see the role of left-wing parties today and do you see any opportunities for other (more radical) parties to play a greater role following the crisis of social democracy? What exactly is the crisis of the left today?

The crisis or defeat of social democracy is only the latest in a series of defeats for the left. In 1914, 1933, 1989, chauvinism, racism, anti-Semitism, ethnicism defeated the socialist workers' movement; also because of the transformation of the economy and technology, the working class (as a political subject) has lost the initiative, is politically passive or has been transformed into an exclusionary right which sees the rivals of traditional labor (women, people of color, immigrants) as the enemy. In such cases, it is often said that the left should stop defending minorities and start defending the specific interests of the majority of the working class. But that is deplorable elitism. The workers' movement was not like this or like that because some preexistent 'left' from outside told it what to do. But because the labor movement was a movement of the workers themselves, they rejected the national framework (like the Stoics and Christians before them), their ally was the leftist intelligentsia – the workers' movement is not a creature of left-wing intellectuals, but the result of the self-movement of the proletariat, which has created its own modern version of high culture, of which we are the descendants.

Currently there are biopolitical movements (around race/ethnicity, gender, environment), the radically bourgeois notion of equality is the organizing principle instead of the Marxian model of human emancipation. The most prominent modern theorist of equality is John Rawls, who was a liberal, not a socialist. Traditional socialism is dead. The smaller radical left parties (such as *Levica* in Slovenia, *Možemo* in Croatia, *Razem* in Poland, *Bloco de Esquerda* in Portugal, etc.) are undoubtedly pro-worker, but their membership and electoral base is mainly made up of young, urban white-collar populations, intellectuals, welfare workers, local council workers, artists, students and subcultures. These subcultures in Eastern Europe are in some cases far from the mainstream, in others less so, but nowhere do they embody the alternative of the 'new world' as in 1917-19 or even 1945. The historical configuration of utopia and the tens of millions of workers – or as it was once called: the fusion of the proletariat and philosophy – has been broken.

Interview conducted and translated by Mark Losoncz

NEW NARRATIVES FOR THE LEFT
Patrick Baert

Patrick Baert is Professor of Social Theory at the University of Cambridge, United Kingdom, and Fellow and Director of Studies at Selwyn College, Cambridge. He is Editor-in-Chief of *International Journal of Politics, Culture and Society* and a member of international advisory boards for *Journal of Classical Sociology* and *European Journal of Social Theory*. He has held visiting positions at Brown University, the University of Cape Town, the CNRS/EHESS in Paris and the University of British Columbia. His research interests encompass sociology of culture, sociology of intellectuals, social theory and philosophy of social sciences. Against the representational model of knowledge in philosophy of social sciences, Baert argues in favor of a neo-pragmatist perspective which promotes social research in the pursuit of 'self-referential knowledge'. His publications include *Ideas on the Move in the Social Sciences and Humanities* (2020); *The Sociology of Intellectuals* (2017); *The Existentialist Moment; Sartre's Rise as a Public Intellectual* (2015); *Social Theory in the Twentieth Century and Beyond* (with F. Carreira da Silva, 2010) and *Philosophy of the Social Sciences: Towards Pragmatism* (2005).

The ongoing Covid-19 pandemic is seen by many on the left as an opportunity to "turn the tide" of the symbolic struggle against both the ideology of market liberalism and the populist anti-intellectualism of the right. To achieve this, the left has to some extent revitalized the language of traditional scientism – as the pandemic supposedly reveals to us anew the "value of science" – with its underlying premises of naturalism,

epistemological representationalism, and "truth" and "reason"
in the Enlightenment sense. In light of your pragmatist affinities,
how do you see this discursive strategy of the left and is there a
more viable alternative?

I am not sure whether I would agree with your observation
about recent strategies on the part of the left; it very much depends
on what you mean by "left" (and indeed "right"). I would probably
agree that, in the last decade or so, center-left (and indeed center-
right) politicians and commentators have tended to embrace
science and expertise rather than question it, but then they have
on the whole always done this and I would not necessarily ascribe
this recent strategy to the left in general. What you call "anti-
intellectualism" has not been restricted to right-wing populism
and I would rather say that it is a defining feature of any form
of populism. "Anti-intellectualism" is a broad term, but it is
certainly the case that a growing number of people are questioning
scientific evidence and expertise, which they see, for a variety
of reasons, as biased or serving particular interests. I think it ties
into a broader dissatisfaction with various forms of rational-legal
authority and, by extension, a broader questioning of claims as to
neutrality and objectivity; this manifests itself in hostility towards
the judiciary, science, some sections of the media, and so on.
Whilst very few contemporary philosophers would subscribe to
"representationalism" in its basic form, it does serve a function
in that it provides a recognizable anchor of legitimacy when
dealing with the larger public, although there are also signs, as you
intimate yourself, that this particular rhetorical strategy has run its
course. If indeed we are talking about strategies towards the wider
public – after all, that seems to be what your question is getting
at – then it might be advisable to communicate not just in terms
of cognitive validity but also to present a compelling narrative
that brings people together. There are plenty of examples of cases
where expert opinions have failed to resonate with, or galvanize the
public. We need only recall how during the 2016 UK referendum,
warnings by several prominent economists about leaving the EU
fell on deaf ears. For several years now, in spite of medical advice
and public interventions by qualified scientists, vaccine denial

has been rampant in some countries and could possibly derail our collective efforts to control the current pandemic. Wheeling in experts does not get you very far if you want to reach a large number of people, especially not in the current context of social media. Rather, as cultural sociologists have pointed out, you need a compelling narrative – one that involves claims about trauma, hurt and injustice, as well as hope and solidarity. Assuming we want to stick to your distinction between left and right (I am not entirely convinced about this juxtaposition as it includes several different dichotomies), I would say that in the last few decades, the right has been more successful in providing a strong narrative. For instance, however much I disagree with the spirit behind Brexit and what it represents, there is no denying that it rested on a compelling storyline about lost sovereignty and about how to regain it – a narrative that resonated with sections of the British public, especially with those who were traditionally associated with Labour but who no longer felt represented by the party. It is not a narrative with which you or I feel comfortable, but for many people in the UK it was. In a similar vein, the vaccine rollout in the UK has been a success with relatively few people refusing to be vaccinated, partly because the National Health Service organized it. The NHS is deeply embedded in the collective conscience of the nation and occupies a sacred status. The whole vaccine effort was a presented as a heroic national effort, subliminally bringing up memories of the wartime national effort in the face of adversity. I am not saying that progressives need to embrace nationalism – quite the opposite – but they do need *a* narrative, one that goes beyond scientific rationality.

You seem to be in agreement with Richard Rorty that societal transformations over the past decades have brought us ever closer to what he called the "post-metaphysical" predicament, a prevailing cultural climate of the acceptance of ultimate epistemic uncertainty, of pluralism and skepticism towards "foundationalist" political (and theoretical) projects. But the developments of the last couple of years, the rise of populism and the birth of what has been termed the "post-truth mentality" in some ways seem like a realization of an "inverted" Rortian ideal – acceptance of epistemic uncertainty and historicity of knowledge is used to justify essentialist and exclusionary worldviews and politics, to propound "alternative facts" and foreclose dialogue rather than engage in it. What do you make of the present moment?

There is no doubt that digital technologies have played an important role in the phenomenon that you are describing and I do not need to regurgitate the argument about how algorithms contribute to the creation of echo chambers, propelling people into increasingly extreme positions – this is well documented. But there is a broader issue at work, one which I touched upon earlier, and which has to do with the questioning of rational-legal authority and, by extension, with skepticism towards positions of neutrality and objectivity. For a long time, Western democracies have functioned on the basis that their citizens more or less trust the neutral and objective stance of a variety of institutions, including, for instance, the judiciary, the civil service, universities and public broadcasting. Their self-positioning of neutrality has never been perfect partly because the underlying culture of those institutions does not match that of the wider public. Nevertheless, the system worked pretty well. More recently, however, there have been several instances that showed that the trust which people had in those institutions has become surprisingly fragile, spurred on, of course, by populist politicians and facilitated by the internet which enables access to 'alternative' sources of information. For me, the fragility of that trust has a lot to with a widening cultural gulf created by educational disparities and with a growing resentment from those on the "wrong" side of the educational divide towards those with educational and academic credentials.

Your positioning theory of the intellectual sphere argues against the "declinist" position in debates about public intellectuals – the notion that we are today witnessing a decline in the numbers and influence of public intellectuals compared to the early and mid-twentieth century as result of technological changes and the "domestication" of intellectuals through professionalization of the academia. Could you explain briefly your distinction between the authoritative, professional and embedded public intellectual?

Are embedded public intellectuals inherently progressive, or are we witnessing the rise of what might be termed "foundationalist" embedded intellectuals, both on the right and the left (you have recently argued in The Dark Side of Podemos *that even progressive contemporary political actors such as Podemos in Spain can harbor essentialist, anti-democratic premises)?*

The argument that I tried to make in *The Existentialist Moment* has to do with shifts in the role of the public intellectual. As you point out, I argued against the widespread view that the role of the public intellectual is in decline because it mistakes the fall of *a* particular type of public intellectual as a decline of the public intellectual *tout court*. It is in that context that I made the distinction between the three ideal types, which you mention. Now, the authoritative public intellectual was dominant until the mid-twentieth century and epitomized in the likes of Sartre or Russell. Steeped in the humanities, these types of intellectuals draw on their considerable cultural and educational resources to speak out – often with great moral vigor – about a wide range of topics without having the relevant expertise or research methodology. My point was that this type of intellectual engagement became less plausible or less creditable in the context of the institutionalization and professionalization of the social sciences. Instead, with the rising social sciences in the middle of the twentieth century, professional public intellectuals came to the fore, exemplified in the rising stature of people like Foucault or Bourdieu. Operating as social scientists (or aligned disciplines), these intellectuals draw on their expertise whilst engaging with their publics. Those professional intellectuals nevertheless resemble the authoritative ones in that they both speak from above, communicating to, not with, their audiences. Towards the end of the twentieth century, this positioning became less tenable for a variety of reasons. In philosophy, both self-proclaimed neo-pragmatists and so-called postmodernists attacked foundationalism. Social scientists increasingly felt ill at ease with the inherent hierarchies implied in the model of the professional intellectual – between knower and subject, the initiated and non-initiated, etc. It is in that context that embedded public intellectuals became prominent, promoting a more egalitarian relationship between the intellectuals and the publics, especially with regard to how knowledge is obtained. Indeed, they were keen to emphasize that knowledge was somehow co-created, even going as far as saying that the intellectual is a mere transmitter or that at some level all epistemic cultures are equally valid.

Contrary to some interpretations, I did not mean to promote the embedded public intellectual – I was simply trying to describe and explain recent developments. I do not think that the shift towards an embedded public intellectual is necessarily always a positive development – it very much depends on how it is articulated. Embedded intellectual engagement is not "inherently progressive" – again, it very much depends on what type of political goals it is serving. One of the issues I have with Michael Burawoy is that he promotes public sociology assuming that it would necessarily be serving the political goals about which he feels strongly (assisting labor unions or immigrant organizations, for instance). However, the form of public engagement that he envisages can be for the pursuit of a whole variety of goals, including those that are diametrically opposed to the ones he cherishes. Would he then still be advocating public sociology? Likewise, embedded intellectuals can serve or promote very different political interests and it is perfectly possible to envisage embedded intellectuals who serve an exclusionist political agenda.

Just one point about *The Dark Side of Podemos*, as you seem to suggest that it represents a critique of Podemos, which was certainly not our intention. Some commentators have seen the book in this light: I remember my former colleague Göran Therborn at a discussion panel organized around the book portraying it even as an exercise in "cold war" rhetoric. That was a gross misreading. Josh Booth and I tried to contextualize the movement within a broader context of political theory and we tried to show the significance of Carl Schmitt.

The thesis about the "decline" of public intellectuals is sometimes also framed as a critique of the "neoliberal revolution," the restructuring of social reality (and the academic sphere) marked by incessant quantification, measurement of success and "optimization" of costs, supposedly aimed at maximizing "productivity" and "efficiency." The rigid reality of this transformation goes hand in hand with a discourse of justification that invokes seemingly post-metaphysical and pragmatist tropes such as "experimentation," "flexibility," "dialogical reasoning" and reflexive incorporation of critical perspectives – a strategy that the French sociologist Luc Boltanski has called "complex" (or "managerial") domination, one that takes the form of simulated openness and inclusion, even anti-foundationalism. What kind of intellectual engagement is best suited today to counter and unmask complex domination? Could you briefly explain your central concept of "self-knowledge" or "self-referential knowledge?"

Well, for me, the precise and perspicacious nature of your question gives away the answer. One of the remarkable aspects of the phenomenon that you are describing is the unintended implication of social theorists and social scientists in this novel power game. It is precisely those well-intended theoretical and sociological reflections on the nature of power that have been incorporated to make new and powerful forms of domination. You only have to look at management courses and handbooks: they are full of critical theory! Academics tend to flatter themselves when they claim – which they invariably do – that their work has a clear-cut emancipatory dimension. The reality is that, once this type of "critical" reflection is publicly available, it can be put to use in an infinite number of ways, and future usage is ultimately beyond the control of those who initiated or propagated the theory. All we can hope for is that we have provided people with new and insightful ways of re-describing themselves – that's what I meant when I advocated "self-referential knowledge acquisition." What they *do* with it is a different matter.

You have argued in Conflict in The Academy *that symbolic struggles in the academic sphere, though they may appear to the public as trivial "storms in a teacup" that have no importance in the "real world," actually have far-reaching consequences for the whole social reality as they condense within themselves the broader societal struggles of the day over institutionalized principles of classification. How important are universities and other academic institutions as places where the classificatory schemes that regulate our everyday lives (e.g., neoclassical economics) are produced and transformed through struggle? How important in these struggles are the contingent choices and strategies of the participants compared to stable determinants (such as "dominant" versus "marginal" narratives, fixed identities and class positions and the "intrinsic value" of ideas and arguments)?*

Let me start with a correction, if you don't mind. In *Conflict in the Academy*, Marcus Morgan and I did not intend to argue that disputes in the academy have significant effects for society – rather they often *express* broader societal issues. The case that we studied – ostensibly about conflict around the reappointment of a junior academic at Cambridge in the early 1980s, but also very much about the import of structuralism and "French theory" in Anglo-Saxon academia – reflected deeper anxieties at the time about social mobility, wider access to higher education and perceived falling standards. However, the main bulk of the argument dealt with the performative strategies used in this dispute by the two opposing camps, especially around claims about purity and pollution. Recently, I read Mary McCarty's *Groves of Academy* – one of her less well-known novels, initially published in the early 1950s and depicting a small liberal arts college in the US – and the whole scene depicted reminded me of our study: a literature faculty, conflict around re-appointment, and deeper divisions about the identity of the discipline, pitching traditionalists against "young Turks."

When Bourdieu wrote his main works about the academy, the nature of higher education was very different from today. He was right to emphasize the autonomy of universities and to point out that this was a relatively recent phenomenon. In some respects, both *Conflict in the Academy* and McCarthy's *Groves of the Academy* deal with what appeared, at least to the people involved, to be that type of self-contained world. It is clear that this picture of autonomy is no longer viable for a variety of reasons. What Michael Powell called the audit culture has seriously transformed our universities, especially with the recent emphasis on the need for impact-driven research. Political interference is rife, most visibly the setting of targets for student admissions of underrepresented groups. Layers of legislation are piling up, stipulating what should and should not be done. I am not arguing that all this is necessarily pernicious – I am simply pointing out that the nature of the institution has changed beyond recognition. Until the 1980s, academics could still operate under the illusion that they were keeping a detached, critical voice – this was always a difficult balancing act, but the current academic setting makes it a particularly untenable for of self-positioning.

You supported the Institute for Philosophy and Social Theory in Belgrade in its struggle to preserve autonomy and integrity – do you consider this struggle as important in the above sense?

Yes, I supported the Institute, simply because I very much appreciate the work that is coming out of the Institute, and I realized, when I visited, what an invigorating intellectual atmosphere it is. I also respect the history of the Institute and the role it has played in the political transformations since its conception. If my answers above came across as rather cynical and possibly a justification for quietism, it is worth pointing out that they are meant to be a commentary on the state of Anglo-Saxon academia – not on the challenging context in which the Institute is operating.

Interview conducted by Marjan Ivković

VOICES FOR THE FUTURE

SOCIETY TESTED BY MORAL AFFAIRS
Marc Crépon

Marc Crépon is a French philosopher and academic, Professor at the École Normale Supérieure in Paris, (where he was the head of the philosophy department until 2018), visiting lecturer at the University of California Irvine, Rice University and Northwestern University of Chicago. The theme of violence, in particular as it manifested in the totalitarianisms of the 20th century, is at the heart of his reflection, which also questions the violence of language, which he has called "the malignant genius of languages." He is the author of more than twenty books, throughout which he portrays a sort of toolkit to expose the methods that enable us to transcend and peacefully oppose violent confrontations. In different works, Crépon shows the necessity of a normative moral cosmopolitanism, with the effacement of real and imaginary borders by social media, that enabled our understanding of ever-present vulnerability and mortality. He is the author of: Derrida, la tradition de la philosophie (2008), Le Consentement meurtrier (2012 – translated into Serbian by Zona Zarić and Dušan Janić 2019), *La culture de la peur, Démocratie, identité, securité* (2008), *The Thought of Death and the Memory War* (with Michael Maurice Loriaux, 2013).

Your book Le Consentement meurtrier *(translated into English as* Murderous Consent. On the Accommodation of Violent Death *with Italian and Serbian editions) is an attempt to present "a cosmopolitan ethics of relations." Does this mean that previous ethics have not been cosmopolitan? How should we understand the uniqueness and urgency of cosmopolitan ethics?*

In a previous book entitled *Les Géographies de l'esprit*, I sought to analyze, even deconstruct, all the various characterizations of popular philosophy produced in the eighteenth and nineteenth centuries. Each time I rejected these characterizations, I was always making the following double assumption: that they always generated violence, and that they claimed to be cosmopolitan. And it is this last claim that I wanted to investigate in *Murderous Consent. On the Accommodation of Violent Death*, aware that the previous book had been essentially Kantian. That is to say, the problem did not come only from "ethics." I only coined the term cosmopolitan ethics to allow for the possibility of a cosmopolitanism that did not rest on a universalist and transcendental understanding of man. Perhaps you recall the first line of *Totality and Infinity* by Levinas: "it is of the highest importance to know whether we are not duped by morality." Essentially, I could graft my question onto his: it is of the utmost importance to know whether we are not duped by morality or ethics each time we make an ethical or political claim.

My thinking then proceeded on two levels. The first examines the conditions of thinking such claims; the only condition is to adopt a global point of view. Otherwise, you always run the risk that the morality you seek to impose onto politics is a particular morality, partisan and biased, even compromised against its universalizing attempt by the violence it carries. The second question I examine in the book are the conditions of cosmopolitics, showing that it implies an articulation of an ethical principle. This principle underpins the whole book *Murderous Consent. On the Accommodation of Violent Death*: it postulates that the relations of intersubjectivity are grounded in a responsibility of care, of attentiveness and help, which the vulnerability and mortality of the other demand everywhere and from all.

How did you come to formulate such a principle?

My starting point was the deconstruction of identity claims, all the philosophical, ideological, and political uses of the first-person plural, *we*: we the Europeans, we who claim to live in this region, we who speak this language, etc. At the end of the deconstruction of these belongings, only one *we* remained, we, the mortals. In *The Thought of Death and the Memory War*, I arrived at the conclusion that we should think together belonging to this world as a common world, surpassing all distinctions of culture, religion, language, etc., although it must be underscored that this vulnerability is very unequally distributed across the world. Nothing is more likely to unify us before the law than this feeling of vulnerability and mortality, whatever the cultural differences that separate us. Ultimately, I set the ethical principle of responsibility for care, attentiveness and help this feeling demands of all of us everywhere.

This ethical principle grounds the intersubjective relation: in the relation with the other, I am accountable or responsible for their care, attentiveness towards them, helping them. Far from depending on some transcendental idea of man, the principle refers to concrete experience, to immanence, which is the lack of such responsibility. Its weakness or fault line manifests in all the transactions we accord ourselves through the universality of its demand, even though it should have no exception. There is no other way to live our belonging in the world. We constantly accommodate violence, shut our eyes and stop our ears, and act dumb. We "tolerate" the fact that there are men and women who are destitute and we accept to live in a system which contributes or at least does nothing to suppress forms of vulnerability and this increase in mortality. What I call "murderous silence" is not merely a division into those innocent and guilty, it is a constitutive dimension of our being in the world. No one escapes it. We, for example, can live very well, knowing fully that on the other side of the Mediterranean there are thousands of men and women dying of hunger, in forgotten wars, that there are tremendous injustices between the North and South, inequalities in available care, etc.

In the years since the publication of Murderous Consent. On the Accommodation of Violent Death, you have published two books that seem to continue the same line of thinking (both edited by Odile Jacob): L'épreuve de la haine, essai sur le refus de la violence *(2016) and* Inhumaines conditions. Combattre l'intolérable *(2018)*. *Could you tell us how you were called upon to write these additions?*

To summarize very briefly, what *Murderous Consent. On the Accommodation of Violent Death* and *L'épreuve de la haine* attempted to be is an articulation of two ethical principles: not only the one we have already mentioned (responsibility of attentiveness, care, and help that result from the vulnerability and mortality of all everywhere), but also, in its wake, unconditional refusal of violence that stems from it, condemnation, without recourse to justification, caution, alibis given in the course of the last century and much before that, which writers or thinkers have tried to find. As for the second principle, it is not enough to say that it was constantly attacked and probed by all those who sought to persuade us that violence is being confused with the real, that violence is sometimes necessary, or that political reality bars us from not using it, and who enjoined us to choose to condemn some violence and accept other, or if not accept then support, at the cost of an unbearable "casuistic of blood."

For me the task is very clear. It consists, first of all, of showing that violence is not inevitable; on the contrary, the historicity of the human condition is defined by the modification and perception of violence, that is to say, the human capacity to identify with, to designate and no longer tolerate its manifestation, for as long as it is being accommodated. It should be shown, in other words, that the refusal of violence is not merely an ethical principle, but that it allows, very precisely, the engagement of thought and action, of politics, which contribute to the shifting of our threshold of tolerance. Undoubtedly, we will never be entirely free of violence on a global scale. And it is even unimportant whether we today live in societies more or less violent than those in the past. What is actually important is to recognize the common work accomplished by artists, writers, thinkers, activists in promoting societies (certainly not all at the same time and at the same pace) to rid themselves of specific violent forms by rendering them visible and unacceptable. That is my thesis. There are at least three examples that illustrate it very well: child labor, perfectly acceptable by the public in the nineteenth century, which felt that it could not live without its benefits – no longer today. The death penalty and cruel corporal punishment, which many societies have learned to see as unacceptable and have banned it as a form of repressive measure. Finally, school and home violence, which for a long time unfolded behind closed doors, hidden from view and without the possibility of the intervention of the law, are now proscribed.

Your philosophical works are distinguished by a broad knowledge of literature. Could you tell us how you justify this?

Literature has been with me in writing all my books. There are largely two ways of thinking about the relation between literature and philosophy. The first turns the philosopher into a supreme hermeneutic reader of literary text, as if they were translating the truth of the text into conceptual language. The risk remains, however, that the particularity of literary work, the writing, the form, the ambiguities dissolve in favor of philosophical theory, which seeks to pin down the meaning, unless it is simply using it as a guarantee or illustration. The other way, inversely, consists of interrogating not the meaning of the literary text, but some function or other it has within society. In *Inhumaines conditions*, I took this path, just as in *La vocation de l'écriture*. Without wishing to determine its role once and for all, what I have done is to try to show how politics of literature consists of rendering visible what we do not know how (or wish) to see, it imagines what we do not have courage to imagine. Literature, thus understood, contributes to a shift in perception of violence, but not in general, rather how through very concrete manifestations it attacks, even destroys, each time in a unique way, the body and spirit of those who face it. This is Victor Hugo's strategy of engagement when book after book, across sundry genres, he seeks to make the death penalty unacceptable to us. His novel *The Last Day of a Condemned Man*, is in this regard, in my view, exemplary. The defenders of capital punishment – claiming its social necessity – do not know what they are talking about, to the point that they did not put in any effort to see what Hugo's narrative permits to imagine. Of course, literature is not alone; this is call to which cinema has responded, as I present in the analysis of two films by the brothers Dardenne (*Rosetta* and *Deux jours, une nuit*), with which I open *Inhumaines conditions*.

What this parallel between cinema and literature allows us to think is what we could call the experience of desaturation. All images, just as all text, even when they seek to show us or talk to us about violence, do not necessarily allow the experience of violence to become unacceptable. On the contrary, the invasion of violence through image and text can produce a real saturation that destroys even the possibility of this change in consciousness or spirit, which is still the best path to raise the threshold of tolerance. Jointly, literature and cinema invite us to rethink the counter-power of words, as well as of images, so that we might oppose the slow sedimentation of the unacceptable that slowly but surely renders the unacceptable habitual.

Let us talk now about your latest book, Ces temps-ci, la société à l'épreuve des affares de moeurs, *which came out in the fall of 2020. It is dedicated to affairs of sexual harassment, sexual assault, and pedophilia, which have rocked the cinema and literary world these last few years, as well as the Church and sporting organizations. How do you see this period?*

In *Inhumaines conditions* I was interested less in violence itself and more in the conditions that allow its withdrawal into a specific domain, in a given society. I do not wish to believe that societies are condemned to certain forms of violence and to which they must consider themselves fated. The raising of the threshold of tolerance always assumes three things. On the one hand, individual voices who show violence for what it is. Then, a relay of opinion movements that deal with the question, building an audience, which an individual voice would not be able to do. Finally, the work of a legislator to translate this refusal of violence into law. In writing the previous book, I was aware that a chapter was missing on sexual abuse. That chapter then became a book. How I understand the current situation is that suddenly, society is wrestling with this question, and that different actors have come together to push our threshold of tolerance with regard to these abuses. The individual voices that dealt with the issue initially were essentially the victims. They were the ones to break the wall of silence behind which they were imprisoned for years. Their impact came from their presenting, with considerable strength, the traumas tied to such forms of violence: either assault, pedophilia, incest, rape, and in general forms of harassment. My impression is that we are living through a dramatic moment from this standpoint: tolerance of various societies with regard to sexual abuses, which until recently they neither wished to acknowledge nor understand the resulting trauma, is currently withdrawing.

It is a seismic shift, a movement that has shaken even extremely solid institutions: the Church can no longer shut its eyes, the art and entertainment world either, just like the world of sport. All these milieus are thus forced to confront their silence and complicity, which are no longer acceptable. Thinking about my children and my students, it is clear to me that it is a decisive phenomenon, particularly remarkable for a whole generation. I do not wish to say that my generation, people born in the early 1960s, had no awareness of the existence of harassment, of sexual abuse, and rape, but I do not think that the awareness of it we did have in the 1980s had for our minds, our engagement, our struggles the same significance as it does today for the generation of my children and students. We were still absorbed by the contestation of previous generations to oppose the various forms of repression of sexuality, family, morality, sociality, religion, which weighed on our desires. What got lost, or was put into the background, is that it could contain (as it still can) violence in such expressions and brutal in its liberation. It seems to me that what has taken place is a shift in paradigm on these issues. The accent has been moved from the liberation of sexuality to the concern for victims of sexual aggression.

How would you define in this regard the particularity of incest,
on which you spend quite of bit of time in the book?

What is terrible about incest is that the walls that hide its secrets
have for a long time remained untouchably solid, and still are. Not
least among these walls is our idealization of the family. It has
been taboo for so long, and has been able to be spoken of only in
oblique terms, because it is doubly disturbing to the image we have
ourselves made and which we celebrate. First, we have a need to
believe – with good reason – that the attachment at the heart of the
family that ties children to their parents and their grandparents,
to their aunts and uncles, and brothers and sisters to each other,
constitutes a force allowing everyone to construct and project
themselves into the future. It appears natural to us, quite rightly,
that education finds support in the trust and love that strengthen
its ties. What incest painfully reveals is that such eroticization of
violence can never be excluded; which is what all sexual assault
consists of, reciprocating love with its opposite, that is, with a
destructive force. Sometimes, probably more often than we would
like to believe, it happens that affection steps out of its frame, giving
license to a sexuality that it should prohibit to itself. What must be
recalled, tirelessly so, is that this emergence is a crime that cannot
be excused. "Initiation into sexuality" for one's own "pleasure"
can never, under any circumstance, be a constitutive element of
education. It is and has always been nothing by a monstruous alibi
given by predatory adults to dispose of children's bodies with the
aim of satisfying their drives. Yet, this is not the only reason incest
disturbs our perception of the family. Why does love break out of
its frame? Why does all too often the social environment remain
silent? Because incest cannot be separated from manifestations of
patriarchal domination, but rather constitutes an extension thereof,
as well as its most despicable perversion. Each unique case
demands a different analysis, so we should not generalize. But
where much of the stories and testimonies overlap is a description
of a "familial scene," in which multiple men, given the power of
absolute domination over the rest of the family, over which they
rule as masters, take it to be their right to possess as sovereigns
their children's bodies. Undoubtedly, therein lies the reason why

public power took so long to meddle into family secrets, however monstrous they were. In the interest of children, it was time to open those doors.

The idea of the end, or at least the decline of intellectuals has been defended in numerous important theoretical texts published in the last three decades. Do you agree with this thesis and what, in your opinion, is the role and function of engagement of intellectual in contemporary societies and social struggles? Finally, you have been active in numerous social movements for democracy and freedom. Recent among these struggles was that of the Institute for Philosophy and Social Theory in Serbia, for which you joined an international appeal of support and which yielded positive results. Do you think that intellectuals can make a difference in society and if so, what kind?

As a matter of principle, I am skeptical of any rhetoric of "the end" or "decline." It favors passivity and resignation, and a form of nihilism that ends up always agreeing to the worst. All the topics we have discussed in this interview, following your questions, prove the opposite: there is still a need for intellectuals to occupy that place in society, so problematic for the people in power. How could we even think pathways away from murderous silence, rejection of the double culture of fear and the enemy that feeds it, the identification of forms of violence that societies do not wish or know how to see, the lowering of thresholds of tolerance that make the unacceptable acceptable, without recognizing the crucial role played by those in society who have felt the calling (that is their vocation) to awaken this "critical spirit," without which neither this new path, nor rejection, nor identification, nor shift of threshold would be possible. Both intellectuals and activists incarnate this work. It is no accident that authoritarian and dictatorial regimes are always trying to silence them – their repression in democracies is still the most telling sign that it is endangered and already weakened. If we are indeed witnessing "the end" of intellectuals, would the political powers that be, even the best-intentioned ones, be as afraid of them as they are? Why then are they worried? If they do fear them, on the other hand, it is because it is the very role of intellectuals to present a counter-power, giving the citizens critical tools to hone their critical spirit. Each time some political power, whatever it may be, presents distrust or defiance against intellectuals, fearing that they might be feeding such a spirit, it proves that, succumbing to the temptation of verticality, it is able to suffer less and less a contestation of its arbitrariness.

Interview conducted by Zona Zarić

IGNORANCE IS A SERIOUS MATTER
Maurizio Ferraris

Maurizio Ferraris is an Italian continental philosopher and scholar, Distinguished Professor of Philosophy in the Department of Literature and Philosophy at the University of Torino. His name is associated especially with the philosophical current of "new realism," for which he wrote the *Manifesto of New Realism* (2014), and which shares significant similarities with speculative realism and object-oriented ontology. With his TV show on RAI 5 and his column in *La Repubblica*, he manages to introduce philosophy to everyday life and sophisticated arguments into conversations on ordinary topics. In his research, he searches for traces in documents and in archives in the era of internet technologies. His short book *Ignorance Is a Serious Matter* drew significant interest from the public because of his statement that humans are generally ignorant. He is the author of *Goodbye Kant* (2013), *Manifesto of New Realism* (2014), *Where are you? An Ontology of the Cell Phone* (with a foreword of Umberto Eco, 2015), *Intorno agli unicorni. Supercazzole, ornitorinchi, ircocervi* (2018).

The Covid-19 pandemic has changed the meaning of being there, being present. We have switched rapidly to Zoom meetings, even schools have reorganized their lectures via television or internet. How do you see this new reality?

In a certain sense, the virus has responded to the already existing crisis, to an accelerative path that has taken over all of humanity, even without us noticing. I can start from my personal experience: previously I had four flights a week, while since the end of February I have not had a single one and have only had a couple of train trips. Have I been worse at my work?

Has my thinking been impaired? I wouldn't say so. The idea that a philosopher can write his books on a plane is obviously a recent one and it may disappear just as it appeared. A lot of communication can be done online, saving money and time. At this point, I recognize two major problems with the Internet. The first is the fact that these instruments of communication are still extremely rudimentary (probably because their use was sporadic), and the second is that if scientific philosophical research can be largely done remotely (after all, none of us have ever met Plato), the field of education is changing entirely. Education is a period of formation and socialization that cannot be done in any way except in person, by presence, and this is largely true for universities as well. Precisely because of this, the solution to communicate remotely is not sufficient and a solution must be developed to maintain a physical social presence, with the hope that the virus will disappear in the near future.

You have been writing a lot on reality and how it influences our ideas. However, we have seen recently substantial rise of distrust towards science and promotion of so called "alternative facts." How do you explain this? Are alternative facts intrinsically connected with Internet as a free-access space for sharing ideas, opinions, and beliefs?

Are you sure that is the case? According to the situation in Italy, there are two phenomena from previous years that were radically oversized during the Covid crisis. The first was a conspiracy, a call for alternative truths, distrust of science. In fact, one opposition to the vaccine (anti-vaxx movement) in an era in which the main preoccupation of humanity is to find a vaccine against Covid, is pathetic and outdated. Just as the sovereign ones became pathetic and outdated, when it became clear that no country can do it alone. And people who claimed to be charismatic and who believed that the power of will, and stubbornness could change the reality of facts, were humiliated and ridiculed: just think of Trump, Boris Johnson, Bolsonaro. The illusion they provided to their voters, a kind of triumph of will and determination, was shattered by the virus. All in all, it went well, because such illusions are usually dismantled in wars.

Our ability to focus has shortened, as you claim. We indulge in short forms – sitcoms, video clips – that bring "true reality" to us. The language has changed, it's simpler, it has to say everything in few sentences. In business you have this term "elevator pitch" meaning that you have to say everything, to sell your project, idea in less than two minutes. How do you see the further development of humanity in these circumstances? And how do you see inequality, gaps towards those without access to technology?

Are we sure that we once had such a great opportunity to concentrate? Personally, many times I had been deconcentrated during lectures and conferences, I happened to fall asleep and I believe that, like every reader on planet Earth, at some point I skipped the pages where Balzac gets lost in describing the furniture in the room. I claim that the possibility of concentration has an essential value, unfortunately a demanding one, which I have achieved with difficulty and which I think can be achieved in any epoch, as long as there is will for it. It has huge advantages, but I was not taught that by the media in my youth, which also aimed at distraction and brevity, but by good teachers and demanding schools. Instead of getting angry at Twitter, which does its job (and reaches out to those groups of people who used to be illiterate, let's not forget that) we need to think more broadly and invest in education.

You have written a brilliant pamphlet on stupidity. Stupidity of others makes us laugh, but it is not that simple and without dangerous consequences. You claim that the true nature of man/ woman is idiocy, and that technology only reveals this fact. How can we make an order in the world, in our countries to limit the effects of stupidity today?

The way it has always been done: by suppressing, limiting, supporting. Contrary to popular belief, it is not true that there are more stupid people today than was the case before (proportionally, of course). I am sure that there were almost as many fools in the Paleolithic caves as in a modern university or parliament. The only difference is the fact that fools in the Paleolithic did not leave a trace, while postmodern nonsense fills the pages and pages of social networks. It is also true that prehistorically stupid people took greater risks, such as avoiding being eaten by a saber-toothed tiger, than the risks modern professors or envoys have to take. It is very clear that civilization on its own reduces the cruelty of the selection process, but I would be the last to complain about that, considering that I do not know how to communicate with a tiger.

Political theorists report a great rise in populism, especially authoritarian populism. Could you compare briefly the situation in Italy and Serbia? The most recent outburst of protests in Serbia was openly against promotion of stupidity, as protestors claim that its government lied to them and treats them as stupid.

I don't know the situation in Serbia well enough, but I know the one in Italy, even too well, and it seems to me that they are alike. I would like to emphasize an aspect that represents a glimmer of hope. It is difficult to find a moment in the history of the world in which the government did not treat its subjects as stupid. Stalin, as an expert in linguistics, Elena Ceausescu as a great scientist, the Pope's dogma of infallibility, the idea that the authority of royal authority comes from God. And they treated them as stupid because they were stupid, or more precisely, they were mostly uneducated and behaved obediently and traditionally. The fact that this is no longer the case today, the fact that people tend to think for themselves, has drastically changed the scene, both in a bad way (populism is the realization of the dictatorship of the proletariat, rulers spend their time tweeting and watching the effect it produces), and in a good way, reflecting in the, once unimaginable, revolting spirit of people who do not seek only bread in modern times, but intellectual respect as well.

What is the role of intellectual in that sense? You strongly advocate that science and philosophy must be accessible and useful outside of school. However, experts and intellectuals, at least in

*Serbia, almost feel overwhelmed by the flood of incompetence.
How to approach this in a proper way?*

First of all, the historical magnitude of the problem should
be taken into account. Power has always had a conflicting
relationship with knowledge: Plato was expelled from Syracuse,
Frederick the Great fired Voltaire... Elsewhere, it should be
taken into account that experts and intellectuals can make
perfect mistakes, no less than politicians; obviously as a class it
is difficult for us to admit something like that, but if over dinner
we hear a colleague talking about another colleague, we will
realize how little consensus there is in the intellectual sphere.
In the third place, the specificity of this moment is in the fact
that science and philosophy have been criticized not only by
tyrants, but also by ordinary citizens. I will follow up on the
previous answer here. As strange as it may seem and as sad as
it may be, this is one consequence of the Enlightenment, that is,
the implementation of the principle "dare to think for yourself."
Unfortunately, the other two principles of the Enlightenment
"learn to think in agreement with yourself, i.e., in a consistent
way" and "learn to think by putting yourself in the position of
others," have not been observed, because they are much more
difficult to implement. But as sad as it is to see a man who speaks
and writes mediocre English, who believes that Puerto Rico is not
part of the United States, who advises us to fight the virus with
disinfection injections, who treats a great virologist as a nobody
– is one huge consequence of democracy that shows that anyone,
literally anyone, can become president of the United States and
can express their opinion on any topic. Let's not forget that when
the factory councils asked for the opinion of a fellow worker, he
did not have the same authority as his colleague Trump, but he
could utter nonsense no less. I understand that this is not a great
consolation for those who are under populist rule, because the
most impressive effect is not so much in the decisions of the boss,
but in the fact that many compatriots end up standing behind him.
From experience, as an Italian, I can give you one good piece of
news: populism in the age of Internet lasts a little longer than the
tweets that brought them to power. Almost exactly a year ago,

Salvini was walking along the Italian beaches, announcing his intention to ask for full authority, waving rosaries and mojito cocktails around. Today it no longer matters at all.

Interview conducted by Gazela Pudar Draško

HOW TO (RE)INSCRIBE VIRTUE INTO POLITICS ANEW
Ivan Vejvoda

Ivan Vejvoda is a Permanent Fellow, Head of Europe's Futures - Ideas for Action at the Institute for Human Sciences in Vienna (IWM), Senior Vice President for Programs at the German Marshall Fund (GMF) of the United States. From 2003 until 2010, he served as Executive Director of GMF's Balkan Trust for Democracy, a project dedicated to strengthening democratic institutions in South-Eastern Europe. Vejvoda was a senior advisor on foreign policy and European integration to Prime Ministers Zoran Djindjic and Zoran Zivkovic. Prior to that, he served as Executive Director of the Belgrade-based Fund for an Open Society from 1998 to 2002. During the mid-1990s, Vejvoda held various academic posts in the United States and the U.K., including at Smith College in Massachusetts and McAlester College in Minnesota, and the University of Sussex in England, and has published widely on the subjects of democratic transition, totalitarianism, and post-war reconstruction in the Balkans.

In the last few decades, we've heard a lot about "European values." How do you understand them today with the rise of authoritarian, xenophobic, and nationalist, in a word – populist movements in central and eastern, but also western Europe? Are these movements an existential threat to the European project?

With the victory of Donald Trump in the 2016 elections, we should also add the US to this rise of populist movements and parties. European values are really universal human rights values, freedom of expression, of gathering, as well as the rule of law, checks and balances among institutions, which is to say the division of power into legislative, executive, and judicial. Freedom of the individual is the essence of these values. Freedom demands a specific normative framework, norms tied to given sanctions and an organizational framework for them. Institutions are essential. They determine the space within which citizens live and arrange all their lives, beyond any transcendent power. Occupying and maintaining the space of freedom is the basis for a modern democratic society. After all, the modern world stands on the achievements of modern democratic revolutions of the late eighteenth and early nineteenth century in England, France, and the US The slogan, *liberté, égalité, fraternité* (the last might today be replaced with the word solidarity) encapsulates the essence of the modern individual's values. Authoritarian, xenophobic, nationalist regimes and parties – populist ones – reject if not all, then a large portion of these rights and freedoms. Democracy is endangered, institutions damaged, placed in a hold and often hollowed out, shells of their former structures or what they ought to be.

The universal values of freedom and democracy are fragile and prone to abuse, and must be continuously reinvented (Claude Lefort) and defended. Democracy is an open system, and therefore susceptible to attack by enemies of freedom. Such tendencies are indeed a danger to the survival of the European project. But what we also see is resilience of democratic and freedom-loving forces. We see an active, engaged resistance to these regressive tendencies.

In recent years, we have witnessed, on both the local and global level, the rise of movements that focus their efforts on gender politics and climate issues. How do you understand these changes, and how do you see their long-term social and political effects?

Such movements appeared as early as the 1960s, especially in 1968 in a number of countries, but in France in particular. The US and Europe have seen younger generations calling the social order into question, scrutinizing inequalities of all kinds, from the position of women in society, gender equality, ecological issues, to attitudes towards mental illness (such the anti-psychiatric movement). These movements developed and struggled to raise both local and global awareness of these problems and their solutions. The issue of climate change is today a crucial question on a planetary level. International conferences, global and local movements – all seeking ways to lower carbon emissions, lower pollution, lowering the temperature of the planet by 1.5 C°.

The feminist movement, the movement for women's rights, the movement to allow women to make decisions about their own bodies, are particularly important, especially in countries with a growing conservative public and conservative right-wing governments. The fact that in a great number of countries, women still have lower incomes for the same jobs as men is something that moves people to protest and to demand gender equality in every respect. This is a necessary struggle. Perseverance will be key in reducing these unacceptable inequalities.

With the growth of regressive ideologies and conservative efforts in a great number of contemporary societies, the struggle for equality and human rights has become a necessary means for the preservation of basic freedoms.

Why should the current candidate countries continue their path towards the EU, given that the Union itself is tolerating and tacitly even supporting the damaging of basic European values by strengthening authoritarian tendencies within its own borders, as well as in candidate countries, such as Serbia or Montenegro?

However strange it might sound, candidate countries and potential candidate countries have no other path open to them than towards EU membership, whatever its deficiencies. Of course, technically, there are other possibilities: they could become more isolated from the world and their surroundings, or develop ties with only one country, such as China (as Albania did in 1961 turning itself into a totalitarian prison state). But we live in Europe and Europe is our homeland. After the Second World War, European states decided to find political, democratic, institutional frameworks that would avoid bloodshed on our continent every few decades. The European Union is the result of these efforts, and has shown itself to be the most successful community of countries and peoples thus far. Just like any human creation, it is far from perfect, has myriad faults, but it is the least bad structure of its type in existence today.

Western Balkan countries are geographically, geopolitically, geo-economically, historically, and in every other respect European countries. They are surrounded by EU and NATO member states. Their economic trade is largely with the rest of Europe and EU members, from whom they also receive the largest portion of direct investment. These countries do not have the internal financial resources to develop on their own – they are dependent on help and international institutional funding, from EU member states, the US, and others. They require extensive investment for production jobs, investment in transportation and energy infrastructure. The example of Serbia makes it patently evident: the overall economic exchange with the EU is greater than the combined trade with Russia, China, and the US.

Put simply, we live and work thanks to our immediate and indirect European environment and our relations with it. The European path leads towards an orderly, open, pluralist society. This is the path that should be taken even if there were no EU, if we wish to be a society of freedom, human rights, democracy, and the rule of law. It is true that for a few years the damage to the rule of law in some EU member states, such as Hungary and Poland, has been tolerated. The EU is slow, but it gets there. It took too long to be jolted and for it to put into gear the mechanisms for confronting this democratic regression. Article 7 of the European Treaties was initiated in 2018, suspending certain rights of the member state Hungary. The European Parliament recently declared Hungary no longer a democracy in the full sense of the word. And the delivery of a significant sum of money earmarked for post-pandemic development of that country has been suspended. Upon the Russian invasion and aggression against a sovereign European country, Ukraine, the EU has given Ukraine and Moldova candidate status, offering a similar possibility to Georgia, should it fulfill a few conditions. For a while now, Russia has attempted to undermine the European project with some of its activities. More precisely, it is trying to show that the EU is not successful in its efforts to integrate western Balkan countries. It unsuccessfully attempted to prevent Montenegro's and North Macedonia's entry into NATO.

In all 27 member states, the EU enjoys majority support, which is strong because the people in these countries know that regardless of their particular governments, EU institutions are an ultimate guarantee of freedom, rule of law, democracy, and pluralism, whatever its defects, and despite attacks and attempts at thwarting these freedoms. EU member states that were in the Soviet sphere until 1989, when the Berlin Wall fell, sought to 'return to Europe', wishing to become part of the European democratic family, from which they were expelled during the Cold War. By entering the EU, and then NATO, they sought to ensure their freedom and make sure not to fall again to foreign control, as they were between 1945 and 1989. For the same reason, the people of candidate and potential candidate countries are also largely in favor of entering the EU. I am convinced that if referendums for entry into the EU were held in these countries, we would see clear majorities in favor of joining, for the simple reason that common sense informs voters that being an EU member means more stability, security, prosperity than remaining outside this community of countries totaling 450 million people.

I would like to add one more thing. There is almost not a single person in the western Balkans who does not have a family member living and working in one of the 27 member states, meaning that the majority of people in the region are well aware of the advantages of life in the EU. Voters have a realistic view of the EU, its defects and problems, but also its advantages, and therefore on the whole still wish to join the Union, regardless of what the polls indicate on a given day.

Do you think that the authoritarian-populist alternative to representative democracy, which has been on the rise across the world in the last decade, has begun to somewhat lose its legitimacy; or is it too soon to speak about this? Can authoritarian populism be delegitimized at all in the usual sense: e.g., due to unfulfilled promises of economic performance, social justice, or "preservation of our way of life?" Or do its resilience and attractiveness rest on entirely different grounds?

The large crises that have shaken the world, growing social and economic inequality, the weakening of the middle class in developed countries, a series of crises, first the financial in 2008, then the migrant crisis in 2014 – have all led to much uncertainty in people's daily lives. On top of that, rapid technological change, that is, the automatization and replacement of persons with machines has meant that lots of people have lost their employment, leaving them fearful that they will not find other work or fall back on welfare. Labor precariousness has also led to a surge in existential insecurity. These are all reasons that drove voters to seek alternatives far afield from traditional parties of the left and right center, hoping that a different choice would bring about better outcomes. In most cases, this has not panned out.

The authoritarian-populist tendency waxes and wanes. For example, recently in Italy, the Fratelli d'Italia won a plurality with 26% of the votes and will likely be forming the next government. But three right-wing parties that previously held a significant number of votes (Lega, Forza Italia, Cinque Stelle) have suffered a massive loss of votes and parliamentary seats. In 2017, the Austrian neofascist FPÖ won 25% of the votes and became part of the coalition government, but soon crumbled under the weight of various scandals. Since then, its popularity has dropped significantly. We have also seen the rise of the far-right Sweden Democrats, who will now likely be part of the government. In France, however, the right-wing Marine Le Pen was once again unable to triumph in the 2022 presidential elections, just as her father was unsuccessful in 1995.

I mention all this to show that there is a counterbalance to the authoritarian-populist boom. In France, there is something called "Front républicain," when portions of the general public, together with movements and parties join together at a given moment to oppose the victory of an extreme party. This was the case in the last presidential elections there. This is, of course, not always the case, but it speaks to the notion that in many cases there is resistance to the growth of far-right parties. Hence their changing fortunes.

In 2020, the populist Donald Trump lost the presidency to Joseph Biden; yet, the extreme right-wing Republican Party is still denying the victory based on millions of votes of difference. The question is whether Trump or someone like him could win back the presidency in 2024. What is at issue is the preservation of the democratic institutions of the US.

It is remarkable that in Europe, such extreme right-wing parties have had to revise their opposition to the EU, since the voters still overwhelmingly support the EU community. Of course, the case of Great Britain was always exceptional, and riding a populist wave, voters took to the polls in a referendum to make Britain leave the EU. In the rest of Europe, however, such parties now say they are not against the EU, but wish to refashion the EU for their own purposes, as a community of nations, as an intergovernmental organization.

In power, far right-wing parties have generally shown themselves less capable than center left and right parties. Nor are they unified in the European Parliament where their differences have kept them from producing a strong parliamentary bloc.

Time will show whether populist parties can hold on to power in the long-term. What will be crucial in this regard is whether basic, existential issues of contemporary citizenry will be addressed or not.

In your opinion, can liberal representative democracy reclaim its previous position in comparison to its alternatives in a more or less unaltered form, as the latest election results in the US and Germany suggest; or do we need more thorough innovations (for example, towards participatory, deliberative, or radical democracy) in order to respond to today's biggest challenges, such as the pandemic, climate change, and the vast (and growing) social inequalities?

Certainly, much more must be done for democracy as a system to provide people with greater opportunity for their voices to be heard, to have the feeling that their votes have weight and lead towards policies contributing to the general good and public interest, that is to say, for the good of all society.

Many modern societies have oligarchic tendencies, where the interest of the few, of the richest 1% are taken into consideration, while the vast majority live without impact on the broader political, economic, and social sphere. The economic-financial crisis of 2008 was only one example of where deregulation of the market could lead the world. The crisis brought back the need to think about the role of the state, the question of whether everything should indeed be privatized, etc. Certainly, the liberal market economy, capitalism, is today's dominant system with politically democratic institutions; but if it has no developed mechanisms for robust elements of social justice, then society begins to disintegrate, to become pauperized. Democratic checks and balances are therefore crucial. Hence the importance of finding new forms of more direct democratic life – more participation, deliberation, even radical democracy.

Historically, when such demands of the people were not met, there were rebellions, revolts, revolutions. People fought for democracy and freedom in the streets, squares, but also through existing institutions. Democracy and freedom have never been offered on a plate. The public voice, the voice of civil society was always crucial for winning and preserving democratic space and institutions. The biggest challenges of our time you mention, demand the involvement of as great a number of actors as possible, and their cooperation. Social movements, activities of individuals and groups, coupled with the existing local and global democratic institutions, all must be engaged if humanity as a whole is to rise to the challenges we face and find solutions.

Once again there is talk in the Balkans of conflict and potential violent resolution to disagreements. We hear highly influential Western, but also Russian media putting forward analyses in which war in the Balkans is not out of the question. Is the fragility of this region a result of national-populist movements, rampant corruption, the hollowing out of institutions; or the inability of European institutions to provide an alternative, a European future for the continent's southeastern part?

I think it highly unlikely that there will be an armed conflict in our region. Unfortunately, we were at war with each other in the 1990s, when all around us were in a hurry to democratize, open up to the world, and become member states of the EU and NATO.

Despite the damaging, often incendiary, nationalist, populist and aggressive rhetoric, I do not believe that anyone wishes or even has the strength to go to war. Of course this option can never be entirely excluded, since there are always some who wish to spill someone else's blood, but I think they are a small minority. Let us not forget that there are still some 4,000 NATO soldiers in Kosovo, the military mission of the EU to Bosnia and Herzegovina is called Althea – these troops are present because wars did take place, but also to prevent future violent conflicts, and we know that these missions could almost instantaneously be strengthened if worst came to worst.

The fragility of our region is a consequence of everything you mention, both self-inflicted reasons and external. However, it is important to repeat that armed conflicts have ceased, that two former Yugoslav republics are EU members (Slovenia and Croatia), four are full members of NATO (Slovenia, Croatia, Montenegro, and North Macedonia). The rest are almost all candidates for EU membership (Serbia, Montenegro, North Macedonia, and of course Albania), with Bosnia and Herzegovina and Kosovo the exceptions. All these countries are in strong and multilateral economic ties with the EU and each other (which is often overlooked). Regional relations exist and are being developed on various levels, even if relations at the highest echelons of power between some of these countries are not good.

How do you understand the relative impotence and absence of desire or ability of democratic political actors across numerous countries ruled by "hybrid" or authoritarian regimes, such as Serbia, Hungary, Poland, Russia, Turkey, and India, to produce truly innovative alternative programs from the ones put into practice by those countries' governments?

First of all, I would like to say that in the big cities of countries such as Hungary, Poland, Turkey, power is held by parties of democratic opposition. This is an extremely important fact, as it speaks to the strength of democratic forces in society, not just their existence, but their capacity to mobilize voters. Of course, it also indicates a division in many countries between urban and rural areas. Soon there will be elections in Turkey, Poland, and some other countries; we shall see if there is a change of government. In any case, each country is a case unto itself, regardless of the similarities in political processes and socio-economic challenges. The origins of the success of 'hybrid' or authoritarian regimes should be sought in the changes that have taken place in recent decades. In many countries there has been a break-down of the classic left-right party structure. Nor should we forget the technological changes that led to the stratification of the working class; previously, these were votes for the left, but the loss of jobs has meant that many of them today vote for the right, or else for new movements and parties. In the most recent elections in Great Britain, the so-called Red Wall, the northern industrial areas that previously always voted Labour, went for the Conservatives. This was also the case in in the deindustrialized parts of France. We should note the very serious demographic problems countries of our region face. An aging population, low fertility rates, significant emigration among the working-age, often young, population, seeking a better, more peaceful, more stable and prosperous life. These are persons who most often individually become part of the European Union, since the countries themselves are only crawling towards EU membership. This means an aging voting population, often siding with populist parties. 'Hybrid' regimes and their leaders often produce a feeling of social security and stability through frequent hand-outs, garnering election votes; this is on top of employment through party membership. Of course, it falls upon opposition actors, movements, parties to resolutely and in an engaged manner develop something to offer voters that would be more acceptable and alluring from what the parties in power are providing. A gathering of a broader coalition might in this way win a greater number of votes. We see in the recent elections in Italy that the left has paid the price for its fragmentation, that is, the inability of the left center to build a coalition.

The world has changed radically, and political forces are in flux in these changes. There were always new political forces or individuals who popped up seemingly out of nowhere to lead their countries, even when it seemed impossible. Denigrating politics or political parties, the cynical view that 'they're all the same' (equally bad, corrupt, dishonest) leads nowhere. The French philosopher Paul Ricoeur wrote that politics has two sides: one of specific evil, but also specific good. Political and social actors who prove capable to contribute to the improvement of life in society, while ensuring basic democratic freedoms, true pluralism, and a feeling that right and justice are on the side of citizens – they are the ones who will make society better. Perhaps this is difficult to imagine, but one of the goals should be to reinscribe virtue into politics anew.

How do you assess the eighteen months of the Biden presidency, specifically in relation to the Balkans? And will the change in government and policy in Berlin mean profound changes towards this region?

American policy towards the Balkans has been consistent, regardless of administration. That being said, the current American president, Biden, and his Secretary of State, Blinken, are among the best-informed politicians when it comes to our region. The key to American policy can be put succinctly: the US supports the EU in its policy of expanding to the western Balkans. The Americans call this the completion of European unification into a peaceful continent. For this reason, transatlantic relations are crucial for security, foreign policy, the economy, ecology, and any other sense. Europe, the EU was able to develop after the Second World War thanks to the security provided by the US. Although destroyed, Europe could focus on rebuilding thanks to the Marshall Plan, and later develop its project of creating an economic community and then the Union. Thus, the US continues with the same policy of unmitigated support to Europe, allowing it to continue its unification; the Balkans have a key place in this plan. The new coalition government in Germany, elected at the end of 2021 and including the Social Democrats, the Greens, and the Liberals, led by Olaf Scholz is continuing the policy of Angela Merkel. Together with France and President Emmanuel Macron, they are attempting to reform the process of integration for potential new member states, which includes the western Balkan region.

The Russian invasion of Ukraine, now in its eighth month, is a tectonic shift of global scale. Nothing will be the same after

February 24, 2022, just as nothing was the same after November 9, 1989, when the Berlin Wall fell. Russia – a nuclear power – attacked a European country with a population of 44 million. Russia has come to resemble its predecessor, the totalitarian Soviet Union: there are no free media outlets, no civil society, no freedom or human rights, people are sentenced to fifteen years in prison for uttering the word 'war' or for raising a blank sheet of paper on the street. For all its many faults, Ukraine has a democratic system and has gone through five presidents, while in Russia, a single man has been de facto in power for 22 years. EU countries, and Germany in particular, have suffered a rude awakening. Nothing will be the same in Germany and the EU after this. Across various sectors of society, but especially regarding energy, there has been a complete reorientation, so that no one will be dependent on Russian fossil fuels by the end of the decade. The countries from this region are all on the path towards EU membership, with all the challenges this path carries. The region has barely 16 million people, a third of Ukraine in terms of population – if it has any sense about its future, it will continue with democratic reforms and establishing the rule of law, as well as aligning with EU's foreign policy, so it can fulfill the basic conditions for EU membership and join the largest democratic community (again, with all its problem, which are many), thus ensuring a more stable future.

Finally, you have taken up the role of President of the Governing Board of the Institute for Philosophy and Social Theory two years ago, you helped relieve the Institute of pressure, for a while at least, coming from the far right in Serbia. Do you believe that academics and intellectuals can positively impact events in society? And how should they struggle against destructive social forces?

The Institute for Philosophy and Social Theory has a special place in the academic and intellectual life of Serbia (and before that Yugoslavia). It was founded in 1981 thanks to the resistance and engagement of a number of people fighting for freedom, freedom of thought and research. With the support of the international community, they were able to carve out the space of the Institute after the Praxis philosophers were expelled from the University in

1975. With the Institute, they were given the possibility to work and make their living. The Institute then became the home of the most prominent humanities academics in Serbia. The reputation it earned in the global academic community, and even outside it, was impressive. Thus, the recent attempt to strip the institute of its intellectual autonomy, to take away the independence of place that nurtured freedom of study and critical thinking – the very heritage of the Praxis group and all those who were in one way or another involved in the broader circle of philosophers, sociologists, anthropologists, historians, psychologists – this attempt was damaging to the Institute, but also to the reputation of the country as a whole. Hence the sweeping and vehement support of academics from across the world in 2020, prominent intellectuals who resolutely stood in defense of this academic and intellectual freedom. It was crucial to preserve the Institute from any kind of attempted takeover by retrograde forces; to save the Institute as a place where critical social thought can freely develop, as a place that nurtures the broadest ties with colleagues the world over, participating as a full partner in international projects, thus representing the best our country has to offer.

Intellectuals, who live up to that name, have always struggled against destructive tendencies in their own societies, but also globally. Recall, for example, that some 1250 workers and intellectuals went to fight against fascism in the Spanish Civil War. Liberation movements anywhere in the world, including the people's liberation movement against Nazism and fascism in Yugoslavia during World War II, always contained engaged intellectuals in their ranks, if also many others as well. However, just as there always have been, there will always be certain intellectuals who lean towards backwards ideologies, ideas, and regimes. Intellectuals can certainly positively impact society, however few in number, if they are engaged, if they raise their voice for the public good, for freedom of expression and freedom to protest, calling for human rights and true democracy. At the dawn of the modern era, Machiavelli underscored the notions of *vivere civile* and *vivere libero*, which is to say civic living and free living as the basis of a free society, in which citizens freely produce the institutions of their society. This right to freedom still applies today, as does the defense of freedom wherever it is endangered or thwarted. The French political thinker, Étienne de la Boétie wrote lucidly about this in his 1552 *Discourse of Voluntary Servitude*. The struggle against all forms of slavery, even political slavery and unfreedom still moves people to action, across the globe.

Interview conducted by Gazela Pudar Draško

LET US OPEN OUR MINDS
TO HOPE AND DREAMS
Asger Sørensen

Asger Sørensen is a Danish philosopher, Associate Professor in Philosophy of Education at Aarhus University, Denmark. He works on academic freedom, alienation, justice, democracy, peace, political philosophy and social theory through emerging ethical problems and a critique of contemporary capitalism. He is interested in the permanent redefinition of the role of the University, and the formation of democratic thinking as ethical and political categories. In Danish, he has published monographs on utilitarianism, sociologically informed ethics, philosophy of science and on the philosophy of Georges Bataille, John Rawls and Enrique Dussel. His books that have come out in English include *Capitalism, Alienation and Critique*, and *Studies in Economy and Dialectics* (2018), which is the first volume of his forthcoming trilogy *Dialectics, Deontology*.

The current Covid-19 pandemic has thrown into sharp relief the shortcomings of capitalism as a mode of production of social reality. What, in your understanding, are the fundamental deficiencies of capitalism as a comprehensive form of social life? How would you, in a nutshell, envision a viable alternative?

"…in a nutshell, envision…" – well, that is a fantastic opportunity to open up a mind for longing and dreams. In a classical humanist spirit, I would like to emphasize the multidimensionality of human and social being, and the plurality of human talents worth cultivating. A viable alternative to the present form of social life must take into account all such dimensions and talents, i.e., activities and ambitions gathered under headings beyond work, technology and economy, including politics, arts, ecology, science, culture, family life, sports, pastime, etc. And all of these dimensions and talents, and the specific activities and ambitions that they imply, should be institutionalized to make visible the societal recognition of them. Capitalism is detrimental to human beings precisely because it tends to reduce to commodities and capital accumulation the incredible splendor, variation and richness of human and social life.

Hence, I prefer to restrict the use of the term 'capitalism' to designate only a problematic historical mode of production, characterizing instead the present form of social life in a comprehensive sense as 'modernity'. The question is thus what how to conceive of a possible modernity without capitalism, i.e., if the mode of production determines social life and social reality at large, or there are other determinants of modernity that can overcome, neutralize or at least limit the detrimental effects of capitalism. And since human and social beings obviously consists of more than production and commodification, the latter is the case. Moreover, modernity has refined the civilization of earlier lifeforms, extending cultural and political possibilities, healthcare, education etc. to increasing portions of the population. Hence, these civilizing effects should not be attributed to capitalism, as Marxist often do; on the contrary, democracy, education and good health are concerns that precedes and opposes capitalism, and the desire for such goods have – I would claim – been effective in varying degrees in various epochs from the beginning of human history.

Capitalism is this unique mode of production that combines state protection of the right to undistinguished private property with proliferation of greed, technological progress and the application of the market and the commodity form to an increasing number of human and social issues. However, concerns like those mentioned have inhibited the development of brute capitalism, even though in modernity, the social reality ruled by such non-selfish concerns have increasingly been subjected to the commodity form and thus been submitted to capitalist exploitation. The vision I propose is that of human being as a being driven by truth, knowledge, ethics, politics, solidarity, arts, fun and play, i.e., as more than the mere desire for commodities and capital accumulation. In fact, modernity as we know it from twentieth-century western welfare states is in itself proof that this plurality of human concerns is at the core of human and social reality, and we must take this as our inspiration. Self-determination, communal solidarity and artistic expression must again be made primary concerns of political decision making.

Although the pandemic has foregrounded capitalism's flaws, we have so far not witnessed major progressive political developments in its wake – the pandemic has not, as was initially hoped, delegitimized right-wing populism or created a new momentum on the Left. The project of Critical Theory emerged in the 1930s in somewhat similar circumstances, out of reflection on the "paradoxical" fact that the crises and convulsions of capitalism in the 1920s did not result in revolution, but in the rise of fascism and its co-optation of the working class. How can classical Critical Theory that you endorse help us make sense of what is happening today?

Classical critical theory was preoccupied with analyzing and criticizing ideological forms of culture and thought under the capitalist mode of production, i.e., the way science and scholarship, language, imagination, arts and culture express themselves in distorted modes under capitalism. The inspiration was the ideology critique of the young Marx, arguing that ideas that pretend to be universal, and thus attractive and appealing also to the working class, in fact often have biases that benefit certain layers of society, and typically the upper layers. As Marx himself stressed in *The German Ideology*, the ruling ideas are often the ideas of the rulers, dominating thought often reflects the thoughts of those dominating and thus their interests. Such ideas and thought are ideological, and what is ideological in this sense cannot be true. On the contrary, put bluntly, ideology is false, and what Critical Theory aims to provide by ideology critique is the truth of the matter, i.e., not merely another perspective. Revealing alleged clarity and one-dimensionality as in fact hiding bias, obscurity and multi-dimensionality, revealing the suspicious roots of what presents itself as something unproblematic, those were the truths Critical Theory originally provided within philosophy and social science at large.

And such provisions are needed more than ever. As it is now, ordinary language has become ideological to such a degree that it has become difficult to argue in earnest for, say, justice, democracy and peace. Instrumentality and operationality, fear and distrust, competitiveness and profitability have become dominating modes of thought, and with linguistic and conceptual categories reduced in this way, i.e., with such a restricted or even false consciousness, it is of course difficult for the left to gain political momentum. Formulating necessary truths and ideals appears to be experienced as uncomfortable and prone to ridicule. In particular in relation to the politics of the pandemic, on the one hand it is striking how easily well-educated people have accepted that their hard-won political rights are curtailed by the social technologies applied by governments all over the world. One the other hand, however, it is actually encouraging to see how people apparently have chosen to trust neighbors, political government and international governmental agencies with the coordination of the necessary initiatives, and that profit orientated market actors apparently have accepted this coordination. We can only hope that this will also mean a general reinvigoration of Keynesian political economy and social democracy, and that we will not experience a quick return of neo-liberal market fundamentalism, as it happened after the recuperation of the 2008 crash.

In contrast to all those who think that the Left must become post-metaphysical and non-foundationalist – the new "generations" of Critical Theory and the wide spectrum of post-modern standpoints seem to converge on this point – you argue that the Left should remain committed to Truth with a capital T, to Reason understood in Enlightenment terms and to bold metaphysical speculation about human nature and social reality, exemplified by such concepts as alienation *and* dialectics. *This "unfashionable" position is bound to draw strong criticism from the above standpoints for being "authoritarian," "sectarian" (normatively particularist) and "Euro-" or "Western-centric." How would you respond to these charges?*

Yes, it is true that I argue to keep intact the traditional normative attraction of classical thick and substantial ideas of Truth, Reason, Education, Justice, Peace, etc. And, yes, in contemporary social and political philosophy, this is mostly considered problematic; in addition to Critical Theory and post-structuralism, political liberalism also defines itself in opposition to what is denounced as comprehensive doctrines. To the charges of becoming authoritarian, sectarian and Euro-centric by adopting reflective realist metaphysics, I can only welcome criticism that points out the particulars of such flaws in my thought. No one is immune to ideology and false consciousness; it is easier to see the speck in the eyes of another than the log in your own eyes. This is why rights to free speech, education and academic freedom are so important, and this is why modern democracies have good reasons to let legislation be preceded by lengthy parliamentary discussions and public hearings.

When it comes to contemporary discussions on the radical left in particular, there has indeed been a certain reluctance to take seriously traditional metaphysical issues such as human nature and the goal of history, and the present post-metaphysical ideology thus inhibits continuing and developing twentieth-century critical discussions. As I argue, however, we have to recuperate both the classical critique of political economy and its metaphysical presuppositions to overcome the possible ideological implications of the empiricist agendas of contemporary post-structuralism, constructivism and positivism, namely exaggerated individualism, superficiality, despair and decisionism. As Habermas (and others) argued ages ago, adopting empiricism and positivism means that you become impotent as a political actor. When you cannot know in principle anything certain about reality, when you are in principle barred from the truth of the matter, then you have no real argument to offer for one political intervention rather than another. In the same vein, Dewey criticized the spectator theory of knowledge, arguing for recognizing the reality of social constructions such as law and education. And regarding science, Alexandre Koyré argued that positivism and empiricism are defensive and unambitious strategies, modestly only suggesting how worldly things are perceived and experienced, not claiming how they really are. In sum, empiricism is defeatism.

All this adds to a general argument for metaphysical realism as the precondition for being able to handle progressively worldly matters. Of course, this has to reflect the recognition that you are not always right in the first place. We are not talking about naïve realism, but reflective realism. That is why enlightenment, education and learning are crucial, that is why we have to criticize, argue and discus. Ideally, all of this teaches us about reality. That things can be blurred by senses as well as by reason has been the point of sceptics since antiquity, and we also recognize ideology and false consciousness; but it is a logical fault to let the experience of one error imply the distrust in everything possibly experienced. Dialectics is the cognitive answer to a reality haunted by conflict and contradiction, not empiricism, constructivism and positivism. Dialectical thought grasps reality in change and motion, and reminds us that things are not always as they appear, and that they could be otherwise. Dialectical thought thus contributes to both the critique of a problematic reality and the hopes for liberation from current injustice and alienation.

The critique of alienation is now again – after decades of neglect – taken seriously in critical discussions of contemporary society. By its social and political nature, human beings must relate to the community that they are a part of. The problem is that capitalism, political realism, militarism, sexism, paternalism, etc. alienate people from realized modern society, and the political question is thus if – and if so, how – alienation can be overcome, or at least be mitigated. Traditionally, the way to overcome alienation was to gain subjective consciousness about human nature and how it is distorted under capitalism, realizing the necessity of revolution, reform, or at least enlightenment and education.

In contemporary Critical Theory, however, alienation is primarily discussed in terms of individual human experience of living a common life in western modernity, experiencing one's relation to the world as defective, deaf and dumb, as a relation devoid of resonance. Such a privatized understanding of alienation, however, makes it difficult to conceive of conceptually the possibility of realizing historically and politically a world without or with only little alienation. However, in the *locus classicus* of the critique of alienation, i.e., Marx's *Economic-Philosophical Manuscripts*, and in particularly in the reading of them by Marcuse, metaphysical speculation about human nature and history are crucial for making rational and reasonable the hopes for realizing a better world. For Marx the critique of alienation is clearly an integrated part of the critique of classical political economy, the capitalist mode of production, and in particular the protection of private property right offered by the state. The integration of metaphysics in political argument is what makes reasonable and rational the combined critique of capitalist injustice and alienation.

You have written extensively on the highly original and unorthodox leftist thinker Georges Bataille. Does Bataille's central concept of the "general economy" have a potential to inform present-day political struggles against the social causes of climate change and the destruction of the environment, and progressive political movements more generally?

This is a difficult question that I have considered on many occasions over the years, and I believe that Bataille himself also struggled with how his idea of general economy could be conceived of as a progressive political economy. Bataille was most of his life engaged in issues brought up by the radical left, but one may say that he somehow sat uncomfortably with regular communist and socialist lines of thought. The idea of general economy stems from a twofold critique of classical political economy that was waged by Durkheim and Mauss. First, there is a critique of political economy for its lack of scientific rigor, being unable to describe and predict empirically economic phenomena and presupposing the completely unrealistic idea of economic man, i.e., the famous *homo economicus.* Second, there is a moral critique of the egoism and instrumental rationality of the said *homo.*

For Bataille, however, this critique has metaphysical implications regarding the constitution of human being. Of his three volumes on general economy, *The Accursed Share*, only the first one relates directly to economy in the ordinary sense; the other two volumes are about, respectively, the constitution of human existence and subjectivity, offering thus a philosophical anthropology. To put it shortly, human existence is constituted by the continued negation of nature through the prohibition of sex and violence that enables work, morality and rationality. This fundamental negation, however, is negated continuously by the transgression and refinement of prohibitions that gives rise to inner experiences of both joy and anxiety. To establish the subjectivity of every single human being, the basic human negation is thus negated, and in this dynamic structure of double negation, the desire for sovereignty constitutes every human being as a subject.

Crucial for this account of a human being is a generalized idea of the desire presupposed in the idea of economic man. In general, economy is thus about the desire for what is missing, and in the perspective of Bataille's general economy, the economics of classical and neo-classical economy can only be considered a restricted economy. Moreover, when it comes to the material aspect of economy, the general perspective implies disregarding money, focusing instead on resources and energy circulation and emphasizing the necessity of squandering accumulated energy.

And this is truly fascinating, opening up a whole range of critical agendas concerning the conservation of energy and nature, but unfortunately none of them offer any links to the critique of injustice, nor do they relate explicitly to principled normative discussions in political philosophy or ethics. Like other Bataille scholars, I have therefore come to the conclusion that the general economy is a-political or even anti-political in its concerns. Still, I am not settled at all regarding these issues, hoping also that somehow there is a way to integrate conceptually the concerns for nature and humanity.

Another area of your research is philosophy of education, including the debate on the nature and mission of the university. In contrast to both the neoliberal (commodifying) approach to education and the classical liberal (overly individualist) one, you argue for a "republican" model of the education system and university. You also follow the rich tradition of defining education as Bildung *(formation), and, taking the cue from Jügen Habermas, you argue that a specific type of "collective* Bildung*" (citizenship education) is indispensable for a robust democracy. What kind of education, in both narrow and broad senses, is best positioned today to fight the onslaught of "post-truth" mentality and its techniques of government (exemplified by fake news, "alternative facts", conspiracy theories, etc.), which seem to thrive not only due to the suffering caused by capitalism, but also because of the limited capacity of the liberal normative "arsenal" to motivate a counter-movement?*

These are also complicated issues, and I must admit that I have been struck rather severely by the apparent contradiction between, on the one hand, classical ideals of universities and science and on the other, the current development of anti-intellectualism in well-established democratic countries. And this may be the reason that my answers may also appear contradictory. When it comes to the collective *Bildung*, I have tried to take seriously that citizenship education by the *populus* often is experienced as paternalistic, indoctrinating and in general unattractive, even by many of those who in principle are in favor of such education. Hence, when it comes to citizenship education, I have in fact criticized Habermas' idea of collective *Bildung* as being too thin, too formal and too preoccupied with resolving conflicts by law to attract the positive attention of the citizenry. Instead, I have argued for a post-truth strategy focusing on culture and inclusion in a multicultural citizenry rather than on facts, science and political principles. Without community feeling, democracy is difficult to realize. We have to create the *demos* by an appropriate collective *BIldung*. In contrast, when it comes to university and science being threatened by neoliberal politics of western governments, I argue stubbornly to retain the most classical ideals of Knowledge and Truth, arguing that such scholarly ideals are best sustained by academic freedom institutionalized at autonomous universities, externally being independent of state, church and market, internally being ruled according to republican ideals. Striving for knowledge and truth is simply the *raison d'être* of university research.

Arguing so differently with regards to the public at large and the university academics may seem contradictory and reflecting both paternalism and elitism, and that is not completely of the mark. However, in contrast to Žižek and others, I do not believe that everything about human and social reality is known very well, and that we just continue our wrongdoing despite this knowledge. In fact, I consider this idea ideological, relieving the university academics of their intellectual responsibility to society. Knowledge is the privilege and burden of us, well educated university academics, and therefore we must take upon us the responsibility of being the elite with regards to providing knowledge and trust the moral and political instincts of human being when the Truth of the matter is presented clearly enough. Academic freedom thus serves Truth, Knowledge and Reason in the most comprehensive senses, and that is why, without academic freedom, i.e., without the possibility to present unpleasant truths, democratic society will lose one of its important pillars.

You were one of the signatories of the call for support for the Institute for Philosophy and Social Theory in Belgrade. What was it, in light of your philosophical and political commitments, that led you to support the Institute in its struggle to preserve autonomy and academic integrity?

For a philosophy student with radical leanings at the University of Copenhagen in the 1980s, the Belgrade Institute for Philosophy and Social Theory became one of the guiding icons. In general, Yugoslavia was widely respected by the liberal and libertarian left for its socialist experiments with workers' self-management. In particular with regards to philosophy, there was also a certain glamour around the famous Praxis group that apparently had been able to discuss rather freely principled issues regarding social and political issues in their international scholarly journal, *Praxis*, just as we heard stories about the fantastic summer school of Dubrovnik, visited regularly by Habermas and others. In those years, Yugoslavia was one of the strongholds of humanist Marxism, contributing, for instance, to the aforementioned discussion of alienation. Hence, learning that the Praxis group had eventually been expelled from their universities and lost their academic affiliation, it was fantastic as a young student to experience from Denmark the impressive level of international academic solidarity. Even more fantastic was the reinstatement of the group, the creation of the new journal, *Praxis International*, and finally, the establishment of a new independent academic institute. Learning last year that this legendary institute was now being threatened by the Serbian government, I was more than happy to sign a letter of support and even more happy that apparently this contributed to a satisfactory solution of the local conflict. I never made it to the Dubrovnik meetings myself, being relatively slow in my academic maturation, and I must also admit that for many years I did not think much about these experiences of my youth. For more than a decade, however, I have benefitted greatly from a successor institution of the Yugoslav summer schools, namely the annual five day's seminar in Prague, and recently in Belgrade, I have been happy to experience that scholarly rigor and academic dedication is still valued highly when discussing social and political philosophy. The Belgrade community of philosophers seems to be thriving, and I hope that it will regain its former international glory.

Interview conducted by Marjan Ivković

FROM SHELTER (OR REFUGE)
TO THE COUNTERINSTITUTION
Petar Bojanić

Petar Bojanić is Professor of Philosophy and Principal Research Fellow at the Institute for Philosophy and Social Theory, University of Belgrade, as well as the Co-Director of the Center for Advanced Studies South East Europe, University of Rijeka. The areas of his research are political philosophy, philosophy of right, phenomenology, social ontology, philosophy of architecture, and the Jewish political tradition. His most recent publication is the book *In-Statuere: Figures of Institutional Building*. His books *Provocatio: Vocatif, Ius, Revolution* and *Violence and Messianism* have been translated into multiple languages.

You thematize a new concept of a research institute, defined as a counterinstitution. The Institute for Philosophy and Social Theory draws on the heritage of the student protests of 1968 and was effectively founded in the fallout of those events. Members of the Belgrade part of Praxis were fired from the Faculty of Philosophy for their roles in the protests, and sidelined into the Center for Philosophy and Social Theory, which will later be transformed into the Institute for Philosophy and Social Theory (IFDT). Engagement and critique to this day remain the cornerstones of the Institute's activities.

The professors of whom you speak probably never arrived at thinking the institution. The founders of this Institute, and those in the following generations, never thought the Institute as an institution, but rather as a refuge, asylum, temporary shelter. They had no notion of institutional action. We find something similar in Foucault: when reading him, one can tell that he has no idea of institutional or collective action, of something done together. This is simply absent from Foucault. There is critique, there is only individual engagement.

I hope you won't bristle at a biographical way of looking at the history of the Institute, of which you were the director for many years. You personally knew its "founders" even before you went to Paris for your doctorate.

For me, the Institute was above all its library, the wonderful library, which I first visited as a student. My teacher and later mentor, Miladin Životić had returned to the Faculty and teaching at the time when I was a student. I recall that he took me and another student to Kosovo in 1990 or 1991. We went there to talk, and Životić tried to engage Albanian intellectuals who at that point had left official institutions and were living and working in a counter-institutional protocol of sorts. We had a meeting with them – they were all former students of his – and Životić was trying to bring them back to the university. They said they had no intention of participating. This is when I had the first flicker of the idea of a counterinstitution. Double institutions are always fecund. Association is a key democratic creation, it cannot be prevented; essentially, the association of citizens is necessary and direly needed for the sake of correcting state institutions.

IFDT founded the annual award for theoretical and social engagement, "Miladin Životić," awarded thus far to Judith Butler, Axel Honneth, Étienne Balibar, Jonathan Wolff, and Maurizio Ferraris. Why was the award named after Miladin Životić, rather than some other member of the Belgrade section of Praxis?

It's an entirely fair question why not Svetozar Stojanović, Mihailo Marković, or Ljubomir Tadić, all of whom arguably had a stronger theoretical output than Životić. Miladin Životić, however, very quickly found his place. How so? Well, due to his engagement, above all against the war. Since few wished to FOLLOW in the tradition of engagement of *Praxis*, a fundamental inspiration and task had to be to select the name of Miladin Životić for his anti-nationalism, his stance against the war, for a unified

Praxis philosophical group, for Zagreb and Belgrade to remain together – lest we forget, the *Praxis* group broke up with the founding of the journal *Praxis International*, because the Zagreb section was against its founding.

The term of counterinstitution has its own tradition, which you uncover back to Saint-Simon?

There is actually no history of the counterinstitution, since it is utopian. It appears to be a kind of a French thing, but Saint-Simon uncovers forms of the counterinstitution in English civil life. He writes, almost in passing, that he has noted that in England, aside from state institutions, he has noticed what he calls *les contre-instiutions*, structures parallel to state institutions, correcting them.

Could you tell us how you see the figure of the counterinstitution?

The counterinstitution develops critique. What is a key word of the counterinstitution: transparency, certainly. What is its essence? François Rabelais invents the Abbey of Thélème, of which he writes:

> "Then first of all said Gargantua," "there must never be walls built around it, for all other abbeys are proudly walled."
> "Yes indeed," said the monk, "and not without cause; where wall is, front and rear, there is abundant murmur, envy, and mutual conspiracy."
> [*Premièrement donc, dit Gargantua, il n'y faudra jà bâtir murailles au circuit, car toutes autres abbayes sont fièrement murées.*
> — *Voire, dit le moine, et non sans cause: où mur y a, et devant, et derrière, y a force murmure, envie, et conspiration mutuelle...*]

This occurs towards the end of the Second Book of *Gargantua and Pantagruel*; of the seven pages, how long the chapter is, six are about an architectural edifice. Transparency, absence of walls, openness, critique, engagement, experiment, inclusion of others, ability to come and go as one pleases.

What are the meanings of the word "counter?" Surely, it does not mean some kind of infantile sulking, opposition. "Counter" is some kind of relation, but what kind?

This is no deep philosophy. Counter is not 'against'. Derrida wrote about this. There is a poem by Walt Whitman, entitled "I Hear It Was Charged Against Me,"

> "I hear it was charged against me that I sought to destroy institutions;
> But really I am neither for nor against institutions;
> (What indeed have I in common with them? – Or what with the destruction of them?)
> Only I will establish in the Mannahatta, and in every city of These States, inland and seaboard,
> And in the fields and woods, and above every keel little or large, that dents the water,
> Without edifices, or rules, or trustees, or any argument,
> The institution of the dear love of comrades."

Completely open, without obstacles or walls, just as in Rabelais. We construct the institution by avoiding sinecure protocols, by jointly experimenting in the institution, by producing in a different way what we call "expertise."

With your collaborators, the other researchers of IFDT, you turn or have turned a shelter for outcasts into an institution. As we mentioned, engagement and critique are the fundamental concepts of this Institute from its founding. What has changed in the interim?

We have not preserved disciplinary exclusiveness. Interdisciplinarity is the essence of the counterinstitution, and another of its key words. Philosophy is no longer dominant; the field of research has changed. Together, we endeavored to think practice and critique on the meta level, construct a meta-structure, engagement studies. We sought to thematize the Institute itself, thereby thematizing practice and engagement as well. From there, it emerged as a crucial aim: collective engagement, working together. Which is why we at one point signed a declaration that was an affront to the government and put a target on our backs. Why? Because with every good deed there are of course followers and collaborators, but also enemies.

Speaking of engagement, what could you tell us about the process of group creation or making a collective? This word, group, is rather important. Is engagement in a group the same as engagement of a group in relation to the outside, to the audience, the social and political public? How do you put together the terms engagement and group?

A group is the antechamber of the institution. First, there must be a desire, a drive to do something; then to do it with others, to identify another's will, turning individuals into a group; and then a group into an institution. Group, joint work is crucial to institutionalize an institution, because the group possesses the *cogito* that holds it together. The *cogito* is produced by the individuals by creating relations among them. Thus, engagement holds the group together and then institutionalizes the institution. To be engaged means to reveal a problem, resolve a problem, it means understanding that life is resolving problems. Which is something that cannot be done on one's own.

How, then, can general diffusion, a mish-mash of various intentionalities and desires bear influence, if I may use this word – because there is no general will, there is no joint project, there is no...Or there are no rules...there are no rules, no cause & effect, nothing that stands at the beginning, from where we all depart together, rushing towards a single goal. How then is this influence on others, those not present, created?

I think or we think that there is something called engaged acting. There are acts performed by someone to move another, to influence someone else or influence a collective. This influence produces the group. Take an architect who delegates their representatives across offices or in an oversight sends them home; if they do not socialize, if they don't know each other, they would indeed work separately and chaotically. Nothing would get done. In our case, there is an intensity, a right of each 'I' to do as they please, but always in accordance with another's wish; when the other has the same right, it is no longer illegitimate conduct, but an activity that will keep us together, bind us into a better relation. It is better for our own free will and engagement to produce the rules, than to encounter rules to which we have to submit our actions.

Perhaps this provides a point of distinction, of differentiation, a characteristic common to ordinary institutions as well as counterinstitutions, which is a kind of primacy of the "with," that is, that the bond and relation comes first. The relation is ontologically prior to beings standing in parallel, simultaneously. Seeing that the institution exists and that it is constituted of connections, relations and their intensities. Where is the mystical place that produces coherence?

This mystical place would probably be a matter precisely of intensity or tension (pressure). When everyone has the right to do as they please, there is a specific kind of pressure. This pressure is a continuous regulation in the construction of the group. The mystical place almost certainly concerns an amount or dose of pressure, before it turns into torture, into the yoke, abuse, etc. It is much easier when there are rules, when institutions have strict protocols to protect themselves from idleness. Counterinstitutions operate differently: cohesion among group members is achieved through reciprocal pressure and stimulating influence.

How can work be conducted jointly? How can another be influenced to nevertheless do what they themselves will? It seems that it is not a matter of imposing a task.

That's the basic question. A child wants to do as it wishes. How can we harmonize its desire to "do as it pleases" with my wish to do as I please? The point is not for me, this 'I' to order someone else around; 'I' am one who wishes to do the same, to be this other who also "wishes to do what they want." This is a question of conviction: we will do as you say if you convince me that I want what you want. This interplay is an institutional game, a movement and development. The development of a group of people working together is only possible in such a space: in my opinion, only those in counterinstitutions are free.

Interview conducted by Miloš Ćipranić

MIMESIS GROUP
www.mimesis-group.com

MIMESIS INTERNATIONAL
www.mimesisinternational.com
info@mimesisinternational.com

MIMESIS EDIZIONI
www.mimesisedizioni.it
mimesis@mimesisedizioni.it

ÉDITIONS MIMÉSIS
www.editionsmimesis.fr
info@editionsmimesis.fr

MIMESIS COMMUNICATION
www.mim-c.net

MIMESIS EU
www.mim-eu.com

Printed by
Rotomail Italia S.p.A.
May 2023